PERSONAL RELATIONSHIPS
AND
PERSONAL CONSTRUCTS

Personal Relationships
and
Personal Constructs

A Study of Friendship Formation

STEVEN W. DUCK

Lecturer in Psychology, University of Lancaster

JOHN WILEY & SONS

LONDON · NEW YORK · SYDNEY · TORONTO

Library of Congress Catalog Card No. 73-8193

ISBN 0 471 22356 5

Made and printed in Great Britain by
The Garden City Press Limited
Letchworth, Hertfordshire SG6 1JS

This book is dedicated to
my mother and father

Preface

> 'Tell me where is fancy bred,
> Or in the heart or in the head?
> How begot, how nourished?'
> *Merchant of Venice*, III, 2, 63–65.

Most people would like to know the answer to Shakespeare's query. What are the causes of attraction, of friendship, of love or of marital choices? Why do we get on better with some people than with others? Such questions have everyday importance when we spend so much of our time dealing with and meeting other people in a society. But additionally they challenge psychologists to provide answers; and a social psychologist therefore has both a professional and a human commitment to such issues.

This book charts the progress of an investigation into the processes of friendship formation. It attacks the problem on both a theoretical and an empirical front and is largely concerned with the specific problem of how friendship *develops*. I have tried to avoid the familiar listing of research findings without the presentation of an integrational or explanatory theory to unite and account for such findings. I feel it is not adequate to leave inconsistent findings or discrepant hypotheses unapproached; nor is it desirable to separate the 'area' of interpersonal attraction from 'normal everyday' behaviour. Rather a theory of friendship formation should draw upon the tools which already present themselves, and it should not *seek* to create new ones *ad hoc*. Thus the book attempts to integrate research findings by considering a current personality theory and a recent view of what 'social man' is about in his everyday activities. I have tried, too, to indicate the fertility of Kelly's theory of personal constructs in an area where it seemed to have a great deal to offer; both as an overall perspective and as a tool with which to tackle the functional relationship between personality, similarity and friendship. I have also tried to convey the feelings which surround any sequential empirical investigations: how the next question follows from the last study; how it takes shape slowly as the previous analysis unfolds and removes its fifth veil; how the results display concord or conflict with previous studies; how the empirical studies are seen to relate to the theoretical position and may gently suggest its reformulation.

In acquiring this view of what research is like, I was greatly shaped by the benign influences which surrounded me during its creation. Chief among these was the support, guidance and friendly but perceptive criticism offered by Dr. Chris Spencer at Sheffield, where much of the work was carried out. His valuable supervision and his thoughtful comments greatly assisted in the completion of this research and helped to remove many inconsistencies of thought which would otherwise have remained. Drs. John Frisby, Jon Baggaley, and Robert Cook offered incisive yet affable assistance in the development and clarification of half-formed ideas. I have also benefited greatly from the comments of Dr. Brian Little, both at the stage of initial interest in the area and subsequently during the preparation of the manuscript. Dr. Peter Kelvin is also to be thanked for his attentive assistance in the latter stages, and for his initial encouragement and suggestions during the conception and gestation of the book.

During the writing of the book, my wife, Sandra, has patiently tolerated my preoccupation and has offered encouragement and sympathy in moments of anguish and gloom. Her desire to have it all explained to her from time to time has forced recognition of the ambiguities of the outlook and assumptions involved in the work.

To other, more distant, but equally important, influences I also owe thanks: to the Social Science Research Council for its financial support during completion of the research, and to the music of Ralph Vaughan Williams which provided the kind of background where contemplation was facilitated and where results just seemed to fall into place.

STEVE DUCK

Lancaster, July 1973

Acknowledgements

I am grateful to the following for permission to reproduce copyright material:

Editions Gallimard, Paris; American Psychological Association; Psychological Reports; Praeger Publishers, Inc.; Holt, Rinehart and Winston, Inc.; Penguin Books, Ltd.; and the British Psychological Society.

Contents

1

Social Relationships

PROBLEMS WITH SOCIAL RELATIONSHIPS

Throughout their lives most people are involved in some kind of deeper personal relationships with other people. These take many forms, ranging from attraction and friendship of various kinds to marital choice. For most people at most times these relationships are a necessary and satisfying human experience whose function is rarely questioned. It is enough that they are part of our lives. For the intellectually curious amongst this fortunate majority the problems associated with such relationships present themselves in the form: 'What is the basis of friendship?', 'Why do people form relationships with one another?', 'What characterizes such relationships?' This kind of general 'Why?' question—theoretical, interested but uninvolved—defines the scope of their concern in the issues.

However, there are many people for whom personal relationships are often surrounded with strain and perplexity. For these less fortunate people there is a deeper interest in the mechanism, rather than the basis, of friendship formation and the hope of training in 'relationship techniques'. The questions are more significantly phrased in the form: 'How do other people form friendships?' 'What is their method of establishing relationships?' This kind of 'How?' question links theoretical problems to practical outcomes.

Yet others are not simply awkward in company but have become totally unable to form these human relationships in the accepted sense. Some deficiency on their part, some missing comprehension or some lost ability has condemned them to lives of isolation and despair. They never even try to begin forming relationships. For these unfortunates such questions remain henceforth and forever unasked because they have acquired a tragic pointlessness. On their behalf we may enquire whether a more thorough understanding of personal relationships—their functions, their mechanisms, the skills and techniques involved in their initiation—may help to create a more adequate therapeutic technique.

For all these people (and for others who do not fit the categories exactly but oscillate between less extreme limits) there are compelling psychological problems associated with personal relationships in general and friendship formation in particular. To what extent is the ability to form friendships a developmentally acquired skill? What form does the process take? How far can implausible relationships be corrected or based more firmly? Can doomed relationships be foreseen and avoided? Conversely, can productive partnerships be predicted? How can people be helped to more satisfying relationships?

However, these problems are not only the concern of the intellectually curious layman, nor only of those who experience their pointed realities. Many members of the community are involved with personal relationships as part of their professional life. Some deal with normal, undisturbed relationships, such as personnel managers, work-team leaders, and teachers. Others deal predominantly with disturbed relationships, such as marriage guidance counsellors, clinicians and, to some extent, social workers. Others such as child psychologists and management trainers have an interest in the development of interpersonal abilities. All of these deal with the phenomena in varying degrees and at different practical levels; all are interested in different aspects of the problem which lies at the root of personal relationships: what is the basis and what the mechanism of particular choices of associate by individuals? The shades of this question will become more substantial as the argument of the book progresses, but its centrality to the issues raised here remains unassailable.

For all its importance, we can offer small thanks to previous generations for their contribution to our understanding of this problem. The wisdom of the ages, as enshrined in proverb, offers us a choice between 'Birds of a feather flock together' and 'Opposites attract'—the one suggesting similarity as an attractive principle and the other its contrary. However, the general approach of the man in the Clapham omnibus does have one identifiable common ingredient: that people possess properties which make them attractive or unattractive to others. There is no talk in this conception in terms of a process of interplay between minds. 'If you have X, and I like X, then I like you' is what seems to be involved. Thus many stories in romantic magazines suggest a Mr. Right who has all the qualities one could admire. He has them; we like them; therefore Mr. Right and our heroine are pre-destined to become irrevocably and satisfyingly involved. Among these properties are good looks. In the film *Marty* the 'hero' complains on these lines: 'I'm a fat, ugly man, and whatever it is girls like, I ain't got it.' This extends the above notion to suggest that the required properties are the same for us all (or for all girls, in this case). There are no degrees in this conception, no room for opinion; the property acts as some energizing mechanism which inexorably engenders the process of attraction.

Of course this notion manifestly fails to account for the patent fact that not everyone finds all the same people attractive, and, as 'Marty' further observes, 'If a couple are going to get married for forty or fifty years, there must be something more than looks involved.' Marriage guidance counsellors would presumably reflect upon their clients' problems and agree rapidly. However, it will be seen in Chapter 4 that psychological study of the effects of physical attractiveness has not been neglected. Nevertheless, both in marital choice and friendship it is usually assumed that some deeper roots for the association may be found, whatever the initial effects of the superficial foliage. For example, Major Bagstock (in *Dombey and Son*) is an unconscionable name-dropper and seeks as friends those whose names are most estimable. This suggestion of the relevance here of the facility for upholding or increasing a person's self-esteem has been studied scientifically too (Walster, 1965). Again, from the Good Samaritan to Sydney Carton, friends have had to be prepared to undergo inconvenience and suffering. Whilst this may appear to be more a component of his *role* rather than a basis for original choice, it has nevertheless been found that willingness to do such favours in the experimental setting may cause attraction (Kiesler, 1966). However, the friendship of Narziss and Goldmund (Hesse) is based on a realization of the complementarity of their natures— the one finding fulfilment through intellect and the other through bodily activity. This kind of view takes us closer to the psychological problem— how far are minds, cognitions, personalities, natures involved in friendship and social relationships? Naturally enough, this question has also been studied and extended by psychologists (see Chapter 4 for a discussion of the work on attitudes and personality in this context). However, in this area, as in others, the contribution of the psychologist is not restricted to his use of professional investigative skills in the extension of such commonsense and literary notions. It is, to be sure, part of his function to investigate particular issues, but he should also provide an overall view and if possible a theoretical perspective. The next section considers his contribution.

THE PSYCHOLOGICAL PROBLEMS

At its roots, social psychology is a *helping* science. It has the task of studying problems theoretically and practically, so that the individual can be assisted to a better understanding of social processes and need not be awed by them. This aim to increase understanding at many levels has its main profit in this context in its possible contribution to the prevention of unsatisfactory relationships. The ultimate concern may thus be to assist those who experience interpersonal difficulties, but if this can be achieved *via* a deeper comprehension of the normal course of developing relationships, so much the better. For example, such understanding might help to illuminate whether disturbances in relationships stem from a failure to establish and consolidate them properly or from an inability even to initiate their development. However, in fulfilling the above worthy general aim, the social psychologist will need to ask questions as well as answer them, and it is important to consider the questions which arise in a scientific context to assist our view of the phenomena studied. They may be crudely divided into theoretical questions and empirical ones, the latter being given consideration in due course, in Chapter 3.

The above literary and commonsense views are directed mainly to the basic question: Why do individuals choose particular others? But this kind of approach loses much from the scientific and psychological point of view, by not attacking several other problems, of which the otherwise most central would be: What is the place of society in the formation of interpersonal relationships? Why do social relationships occur at all? In a sense, this thought emphasizes the central *functional* importance which the breakdown of personal relationships has for individuals. As Quaker prison-reformers found to their dismay, separation of prisoners into solitary confines ('so that they did not meet other prisoners and spread wickedness or pass on criminal ideas') had a devastating effect on the prisoners' behaviour and promoted considerable ingenuity in desperate attempts at mere communication. Thus it seems that society serves some very important function, and this must be considered in any friendship study, before one investigates particular choices within the society. 'Why do we form social attachments at all?' is logically prior to 'How do we form particular social attachments?' It therefore remains for the researcher to indicate the functional ties between 'gregariousness' (or why we want to associate with other men) and 'interpersonal attraction' (or why we select particular others from the mass of the total population). The question is raised here and attacked directly in the next section.

The raising of this question also has the effect of indicating that psychological study of social relationships can be directed down several routes. Interactions on the formal and superficial levels (where we react more in terms of agreed social rules, formality and 'politeness' rather than in terms of a deeper knowledge of the other) may be of interest to the research psychologist just as much as the interactions of a deeper sort. Indeed, the problem of how one kind is transmuted into the other is of immense importance to the central theme of this book and will gradually become the major concern: How do we get to know people? What do we get to know? This kind of question focuses attention more on the levels of friendship which occur than on the underlying causes of gregariousness or particular selection.

Indeed, there are several other questions which the psychologist may add to those supplied by commonsense enquiry. The business of psychology has often revolved around explanation of behaviour in terms of motivation and personality. Clearly the above suggestion of functional links between levels and degrees of relationship raises the question of a motivational explanation for these levels. What motives make men seek out others' company and what makes them select particularly? Can these motives be understood in terms of personality and phrased within the logic of a particular theory? Personality theories do not, of course, direct themselves specifically to friendship formation. They are about normal everyday processes, and it behoves the enquirer to pay attention to this. For why should we assume that people abandon their normal processes when they start forming a friendship? It is unwise to invest man with 'dual rationality' and thus it is undesirable to regard any particular conceptual processes of man as utterly distinct from his processes as a whole. Just as the psychologist does not cease to be a human when, resplendent in white coat and horn-rimmed spectacles, he walks through the door marked 'Laboratory', neither does man cease to be enshrouded in his cognitive processes when he concentrates on a particular aspect of his world. After considering such processes in general below, it is perhaps more valid to make the claims advanced later (Chapter 4) that processes involved in friendship formation are to be seen as closely allied to those in person perception and that the whole is not to be divorced from personality, or from a theory of 'social man's' other aims in social behaviour. For this reason some closer attention must be paid below to 'normal processes' and to a theory of personality which describes them in a unique way. This theory is also associated with an empirical methodology which may prove useful in the study of some of the theoretical issues raised so far.

Indeed it will be argued that this methodology and its rationale offer us the means of solving a most puzzling problem which research in interpersonal attraction has unearthed. Why should it have been found that attitude similarity on the one hand leads to increased attraction while personality similarity on the other hand appears to have no unequivocal effects? 'Attitudes' and 'personality' are concepts used by both the layman and the psychologist to summarize people's mental characteristics, and this is what creates the problem. Are they not both 'cognitive' attributes which might reasonably be supposed to have *similar* effects? Chapter 4 is the place to consider this problem in more detail and in a more qualified manner, but it is a further example of the problems a psychologist must tackle, and which may cause as much surprise to the layman as it does to the student of attraction.

If part of the task involved here is to chart the progress of normal friendship, and to isolate places where it may break down, then one wants to know whether friendship develops through 'stages' in a characteristic manner. Equally, the explanation of the decay and deterioration of established relationships (rather than the original failure to establish them) is a

Table 1.1. Problems for friendship theories

Mainstream theoretical problems:
  (1) Why do social relationships occur at all? What is the function of 'gregarious-
      ness' and 'affiliation'?
  (2) What is the basis of the particular choices which individuals make within the
      total population? Why do we choose our own particular friends?
  (3) How can explanations of 'everyday' general behaviour be extended to friend-
      ship? Is it necessary to invent special terms and special concepts to explain
      friendship?
  (4) Can friendship be explained in terms of a theory of personality?
  (5) What is the basis of the different degrees and levels of friendship which are
      observed (e.g. attraction, acquaintance, marital selection, etc.)?
  (6) Is friendship formation a *process* characterized by changing emphases or
      different mechanisms?

Some empirical issues:
  (1) What causes the *breakdown* of friendship?
  (2) Why is there a discrepancy between the success of attitude-similarity studies
      and personality-similarity studies reported in the literature?
  (3) Can eventual friendships be predicted on the basis of information available
      after a first meeting? Can doomed relationships be pinpointed before they
      have formed?

---

crucial issue. It bears clearly on problems such as the breakdown of
marriage and has a very significant relation to real life. However, this
problem has rarely been attacked with the vigour directed towards both
original failure to establish relationships and also prediction of satisfactory
relationships.

It has now been possible to isolate some issues which are central to the
present concern. A more detailed analysis of them follows in subsequent
chapters as a fuller exposition of related empirical issues makes their
significance apparent. However, there remain in abeyance the central issues
of the relationship between 'gregariousness' and friendship formation; a
discussion of man's normal processes; and the theory of personality which
is to be adopted, along with its particular methodology.

A BACKGROUND FOR SOCIAL RELATIONSHIPS

In essence, this section addresses itself to the problem of a function
which members of the community serve for the individuals in it. In so
doing, it considers his normal processes and relates the behaviour of
individuals as members of society willy nilly to their behaviour as members
of strictly 'chosen' groups or dyads. It also functions to isolate man as an
hypothesizer, categorizer and evaluator, all of which introduce a theoretical

basis for the selection of Kelly's (1955) theory of personal constructs as the personality viewpoint which is most valuable here. In essence, this theory takes the view that man in general is as rational as a scientist in particular and attempts to understand the world in a similar way; namely, by erecting predictive hypotheses about it and testing them out. The theory will be given more detailed consideration in the next chapter, when some of its value has been clarified. Of course, it is not as such a 'friendship theory', but it can readily become a component of one because of the way in which it treats of man's everyday activities.

Social behaviour can be seen as having several functions and psychologists have offered very varied explanations. Individuals have been claimed (Argyle, 1967) to serve themselves by means of society; conversely, it has been suggested that they subordinate themselves to the general requirements of society (Campbell, 1965); and again, it has been suggested that social behaviour is best understood as an end rather than a means to an end (Secord and Backman, 1964). Clearly such apparent diversity of interpretation is a refreshing testimony to the ingenuity of psychologists pursuing their art. But it is more than this, for in microcosm, the variety of interpretations for a single proposal by psychologists mirrors the variety of interpretations which are encountered in everyday life for the phenomena which are of concern there. Psychologists are also, in more than the strictly trivial sense, examples of human beings (Mair, 1970, provides a discussion of some implications which this claim may have for the conduct of experiments). As such, their work sometimes illuminates the descriptive styles, semantic techniques and logical assumptions of the 'man in the street'. Sometimes the man in the street happens to be a psychologist! This was one of Kelly's points, but he inverted the emphasis of the equality: man is a scientist. What implications can be read into this? If we accept the propensity of man to 'interpret' (see below, for the experimental evidence for this assumption), what view does this suggest about social behaviour?

Of course, social behaviour can be seen to have several *simultaneous* functions, depending on the level of approach with which one is concerned. The problem of 'levels' will be a recurring theme and is not common solely to this area. For example, the question: 'Why did he stop at the traffic lights?' can be answered by : 'Because it was red and he knew the law', or 'Because he saw it was red and he braked', or 'Because he saw a police car in the mirror', or 'Because he put his foot on a pedal which created pressure in an hydraulic system, leading to the application of a friction pad to a moving surface', etc. So, too, the question: 'What is the function of social behaviour?' can be answered at several levels (e.g. 'To protect the species', 'To provide us with companions', 'In order to distribute work and duties', etc.). In both examples the answers are not entirely mutually exclusive, but the appropriateness of the answer depends on the level of the question. Therefore, the present account looks at social behaviour from one level, without denying the validity of others; they are just not our concern.

Put simply, consideration is now to be given to consequences of being a social animal in a group which uses language, and this view will be seen to have links with the position of the 'symbolic interactionists'. Broadly speaking, this view 'emphasizes the symbolic or communicative aspects of human behaviour plus the importance of social structure ... Interaction between and among humans is viewed as symbolic interaction ... Their membership in given social groups or structures makes them carriers of sets of symbols—otherwise known as beliefs, attitudes, perspectives, and so on.' (Lindesmith and Strauss, 1969, p. 8.) The implication of this statement of the position is that, in some senses and at some levels, an individual's thinking is done for him by virtue of the fact that he is (or rather, finds himself to be) a member of a larger group which expresses itself in particular ways. Whorf (1956) has claimed that language itself can impose particular ways of thought on its speakers and thus limits them to an extent. However, while this may be so, and while it is at one level a problem of interest to the psychologist, the level which may be of greatest concern to him is specifically that where individuals make value judgements and hold beliefs which are not pale, 'automatic' consequences of his membership in society. But the links between this 'automatic' process and the occasions where it is more consciously pursued are nevertheless valuable in an overall explanation.

In this account, our particular interest is with the evidence which society provides for the 'correctness' of otherwise unevaluable opinions, beliefs or sentiments, especially those which man necessarily arranges in the process of predicting and understanding his environment, 'the world' and other people. For his convenience in completing this perpetual task, man has become a seeker after order (in the sense of 'arrangement'). By creating order man is able to make his world predictable and is thus able to make his environment more tractable and comprehensible. The essence of this type of ordering is its dependence on a personal system of values (Kelvin, 1970) which, since they are personally established, can vary between individuals or between instants for a particular individual. For example, 'apples' can be classified as 'the fructations of the ovaries of *Pyrus malus*' by a botanist, or as 'highly desirable edible objects' by a starving man. Similarly, the emphasis placed on either classification might change for a botanist as he began to feel hungry. It is clear that there will be occasions when people generally will agree upon classifications; and yet others when there will be more divergence of opinion. However, even agreed classifications are simply a form of convenient shorthand, and a necessary form, which makes communication possible. But the described objects can be shuffled into any 'class' with its arbitrary criteria for membership, since they do not *possess* the properties ascribed to them. The ascriptions are purely for linguistic convenience and our cultural agreement upon them just makes social intercourse easier for us. When all the members of a society have this kind of agreement the question of the validity of a particular classification seldom arises. 'Those' are 'eggs', and that's that. In these cases, by using a common language, the individual employs particular rules for testing the correctness of his classifications and needs to go no further than the dictionary. But in other cases it is not enough that he expresses himself in a language that is shared. What about opinions? What about descriptions of other people's motives and psychological properties?

This broad dichotomy may be related to a distinction sometimes made in psychology between 'objective' and 'social' reality (Festinger, 1950; 1954). The latter concept refers to cases where 'correctness' can be measured only against others (e.g. if I wish to verify that I am a good athlete; or if I wish to know whether my opinion on racial prejudice is a 'good' one), whereas in the former there are objective criteria for correctness (e.g. if I wish to verify that I can jump over a 5' 6" bar; or if I claim that a piece of string is 9" long). In Festinger's dichotomy, 'social' reality may be seen to take its being from consensus. One way in which opinions can be verified, on this view, is by seeking the agreement of other people. They cannot be checked in an objective encyclopaedia of opinions. It is true that many books have tried to assume this function (from the Bible, to the *Thoughts of Chairman Mao*, to *Robinson Crusoe*!), but of course, any such claim would be essentially self-defeating and depends on the consensus which it claims to replace. In other words, its effect depends on agreement that the authority is the Bible or whatever.

But a similar process is also at work in the case of 'objective reality', and it is here that we can test the earlier claim to link social processes as a whole to friendship in particular. For just as the authority of the Bible depends on consensus, so too does the use of objective standards, such as lengths and weights and money values (witness decimalization in Britain in 1971). These depend on 'conjoint community of functional use' (Dewey, 1938). Thus, at a crude level, the distinction between 'objective' and 'social' reality can be seen to fail, inasmuch as both depend ultimately on consensus. It is just this dependence which is claimed here to lie at the root of social relationships. On the one hand, men are gregarious because predictability of the world, at a gross level, is facilitated and secured by consensus; on the other hand, men choose individual friends because they verify by consensus some of the finer components of their outlook—especially their opinions about other men.

At this stage and in this context it is useful to point out several levels at which the reliance on consensus intrudes. Later, and in a different context

(Chapter 12) it will be argued that these levels offer a basal 'model' of social relationships and indicate levels of understanding of other people. The present discussion of man's symbolic activities points up varying kinds of reliance on consensus. In summary, these are:

1. Purely social (opinion);
2. Social-comparative ('Am I a good athlete?' where one compares oneself —rather than one's opinions—with others);
3. Cultural-normative (where one accepts convenience-rules on lengths, breadths, etc.);
4. Linguistic (where one accepts a language's conventional prescriptions: e.g. 'These are "eggs" ');
5. Objective (where one accepts that the object is there at all to be described, as when we agree that hallucinations are not 'there').

In addition, one could add that a 'social reality' of another kind is created every time we accept a 'fact' without checking it for ourselves.

These several kinds of reliance on consensus illustrate its pervasive influence and make the way clearer for an understanding of how it can be seen to apply to several kinds of social relationships. These can be seen to be determined by the kind of thing *about which* the parties demonstrate consensus. The above list begins with topics where contention is more usual and ends with items where a broad base of agreement would be expected, even between members of different cultures (or even different planets). The more contentious the item about which the parties agree, the more personal the relationship and the deeper the friendship. It can be claimed that the most contentious kind of thing about which one requires 'proof' is one's descriptions of other persons and one's attempts to understand their psychological characteristics. A considerable amount of time is spent on this issue in the empirical studies described here and it is important to discuss why this view is taken.

Descriptions of others are often erroneously tinged with a belief or supposition that the person described is in reality a possessor of the attributed property. In other words, it is often felt very strongly that reality is being described, and that properties 'jump out' at us, rather than being imposed by the labeller. People often ask such questions as 'Who was the *real* Napoleon? What was he really like?' But this feeling of reality is just as misplaced here as in the labelling of objects. Again, disagreement by historians about Caesar's motives is not just dependent on the impossibility of time travel but also on the diversity of perspectives which can be applied (even by contemporaries) to the activities of an individual. How does this diversity arise? The central problem, of course, is that we can't see inside people's minds. We have to infer. In so doing, we need to supply a kind of description in order to predict subsequent activity. Thus, instead of saying 'he gnashed his teeth' *and* 'his face was red' *and* 'he opened his eyes wide and stared', we would infer 'He was angry' or we may infer 'He was an epileptic'. These inferences would allow us to distinguish between the prediction 'He will slam the door' and 'He will fall to the ground in a fit'. But this need to supply 'intervening variables' to account for outward bodily signs and behaviour, obviously and necessarily renders our inferences insecure. We can't test them by opening somebody's head. We can't effectively test them by just making predictions (because these would have to be too precise, and how would we know if we were right?). What we *can* do is compare our psychological descriptions with those made by others. Thus it is particularly important for individuals in a society to seek others who can validate their general approach to the explanation of others' behaviour (see Chapters 3 and 4).

SUBJECTIVE INTERPRETATION OF 'OBJECTIVE' PHENOMENA

The main features of the theoretical position as presently expounded are these: that man is characterized by hypothesis and interpretation; and that, in the face of difficulties in evaluating such beliefs, he seeks to validate them by comparing them with those of others. The subtlety of these comparisons has already been hinted at. However, it is necessary to show how much evidence there is for this suggestion and to consider a personality theory which accounts for this propensity of man. In order to clarify this point, consideration must first be given to evidence from many areas of psychology and then to the logical basis of a theory of personality in the light of the evidence.

There has been a considerable amount of research on the problem of subjects' interpretations of that which experimenters had taken to be 'objective' and fixed; and most of this has taken the form of investigating 'demand characteristics' (Orne, 1962) and meta-experiments, but it would be a mistake to regard the results as having no implications for 'the outside world'. Perhaps, also, a profitable extension of this view is that other areas not explicitly investigating this topic can cast light on the same problem.

The early research in this context (Orne, 1962; Rosenthal, 1963) concentrated on the effects which an experimenter's understanding of the experimental hypothesis could have on the results which he obtained. Thus (Rosenthal and Fode, 1963) it has been found that 'experimenters' who time rats in a maze 'find' that the rats do run faster, if they believe they *will* do so, while those who have been told to expect slower speeds will find them. Rosenthal, Freedman and Kurland (1966) extended such findings to the effects which an experimenter's knowledge of the hypothesis may have on his technique of reading the instructions to subjects and affected such things as reading time, glancing, smiling, etc., in a degree found to correlate with subjects' bias scores. The effects and several dangers which afflict any person-to-person experimental setting in this way, have been widely discussed and studied (Rosenthal and Rosnow, 1969). The view that the effects may be due to subjects' desire to be positively evaluated by the experimenter, has been advanced by Rosenberg (1965), and this leads one to suppose that the effects can be, to some extent, attributed to subjects' desire to understand the experimental situation, to put some meaning on it, and to respond 'appropriately'. Schultz (1969) argues that subjects enter the laboratory often apprehensive, resentful, bored, expecting to be deceived and on the look-out for clues to the 'real intentions' of the experimenter—a point reiterated by Rychlak (1970) who urges treating subjects not as organisms but as people, with views and interpretations.

Indeed, it is now implicit in a good deal of work just how important is the subject's view of a situation. In the field of altruism, Latané and Darley (1968) have argued that failure to intervene in emergencies can often be seen to be due to the ambiguity of the situation, which the subject cannot define to his own satisfaction. In many cases, the question: 'Is this an emergency or not?' can be clarified by the subject's observation of bystanders, who can offer some definition for him. If they remain passive, he may tend to assume that the situation is not an emergency. Of course, it is not only likely but quite probable that in some cases the subject is able to remember his own position and to define the situation as 'an experiment', where intervention may be regarded as not necessary, less urgent, or a sign of gullibility. Macaulay and Berkowitz (1970) recognize that in the study of altruism the subject's perception of that which has previously been taken to be a completely objective situation, is of prime importance in determining his actions in it. Allen and Levine (1969) demonstrate a similar view in their discussion of conformity, suggesting that subjects expect different types of behaviour from other subjects in conformity situations as a function of the type of material with which they work. Thus, consensus was apparently expected by subjects on perceptual tasks, so that a dissenter from the majority verdict in a group of observers will tend to decrease the credibility of the group as a reference point. However, no consensus was expected on items of evaluation or opinion, since subjects tended to suppose that there would be variety; so that a dissenter *increases* the group's credibility. Jones, Stires, Shaver and Harris (1968) investigated a more explicit case of such effects, finding that different bystanders made different interpretations of a person doing the same thing in the presence of all of them together, and these depended on the information which had been given to the bystanders about the person observed.

The natural extension of these findings is that the context of performance makes a considerable difference to the way in which an act is interpreted; and support for this view is readily available. DeCharms, Carpenter and Kuperman (1965) provide support for this statement. They report that such gross differences can be occasioned that, in certain conditions, the same act can be interpreted as performed from free will or under duress, depending on the 'information' which a given observer is allowed to absorb about the actor's past behaviour. Briscoe, Woodyard and Shaw (1967) similarly found that negative first impressions are harder to change than positive ones and hypothesized that this may be because negative characteristics are seen as deeper-rooted than positive ones. Koenig (1971) suggests that the greater differentiation observed in the application of negative trait-words is due to the fact that individuals in our society may usually expect to have to give reasons for evaluating someone negatively, while the basis for a positive evaluation is not normally asked for. In other words, both sets of above results suggest that not only the impression formed but also its significance is dependent on the cognitive structure imposed by the observer.

This is extended by Farina, Allen and Saul (1968) who have shown that a subject's belief that a confederate has a negative impression of him will affect his *behaviour*, even when there is no such negative impression initially in the confederate's mind. So, even behaviour itself can be shown experimentally to depend, to an extent, on the interpretation which the individual makes of an 'objectively definable' situation. Furthermore, Ellsworth and Carlsmith (1968) report that even such a well-studied phenomenon as eye-contact has no set 'meaning' but assumes different overtones depending on such factors as intimacy of material being discussed. This once more illustrates that it is not the thing itself but its *assumed* character which is of importance.

In view of these several experimental findings on the influences of context of activity, it is clear that subjects in experiments do not regard situations as 'tabulae rasae' and without assumptions. Indeed, it is clear that it is the subject himself who frequently dictates what a context is rather than the experimenter. In other words, subjects often appear to see certain experimental situations as related to phenomena which the experimenter had not intended to be related; in particular, the situation of just 'being in an experiment' provides a context for some subjects in which to evaluate the acts, aims and instructions of the experimenter. This presents problems for the area of interpersonal attraction, just as for any other area, and these will be discussed more fully in Chapters 3 and 4.

However, in view of what has been said earlier, it is important *not* to see these interpretative acts as things which occur only in the laboratory. They have most frequently been measured there, but are not solely its prerogative. Indeed, there is some evidence that the same processes occur in the everyday assessments of others. Ehrlich and Lipsey (1969) conclude that the impression formation stage of interpersonal attraction is the part where stylistic perceptual differences may be most apparent; and Wright (1965, 1968) has argued that into each interaction individuals take their own particular expectancies and personality 'theories'. It is therefore naive to assume 'affective neutrality', or that values, etc., are cast aside and begun afresh for each new acquaintance.

The convergence of these several areas in social psychology towards the adoption of this same view may be an indication of a greater generality of this phenomenon of subjective interpretation than was at first feared! It may also point to a need for assuming that subjects show continuity of process from real-life to the experimental situation, just as the psychological experimenter himself does. In this case, it would be an advantage to begin study of friendship by using a formally stated personality theory which uniquely embodies this emphasis on man's interpretative penchant. Kelly's (1955, 1969) theory of personal constructs is concerned with emphases which are very similar to those previously discussed, and it is possible to take the view that this theory permits a similar interpretation of the basic social processes. Some of its argument will need to be reconsidered, and some parts of its outlook adapted in order to relate it to friendship formation (an area which it does not otherwise address explicitly). However, Kelly's general standpoint has been well documented in the literature (Kelly, 1955, 1958, 1962, 1969, 1970; Bannister and Mair, 1968; Bannister, 1970; Bannister and Fransella, 1971) and the aim here will therefore be directed more by relevance to the argument than by exhaustiveness. This said, the intention to concentrate on relevant parts must not be allowed to obscure the overall 'philosophy' of the theory, for it is here that the theory has much to offer the present view. For the theory firmly rejects any notion that man is led by the nose through life by 'motives' or by stimuli and responses. The position rests on this fundamental assumption: that events, facts, things, objects and all the paraphernalia of existence have no absolute meaning or particles of an absolute truth attached to them. Men, or other sentient beings, can impose on events, facts, etc., whatever categorizations, meanings, labels, rules or laws they choose—and they must accept responsibility for their choices. The categories, etc., come from the categorizer and not from the objects which he perceives; and, in the light of his experience, the observer may change his descriptions of objects to suit himself. Kelly used the term *'constructive alternativism'* for the view that categorizations, meanings, etc., may vary not only between perceivers but also on different occasions for the self-same perceiver.

It may already be clear that by making our most fundamental perceptions and comprehensions into judgements and beliefs, this view emphasizes the subtle ways in which reliance on social reality may permeate our lives. For if our very fabric of meaning depends on our own interpretation and belief, then we will frequently be confronted with the need to validate these beliefs. Clearly this fabric of meaning, this embodiment of our predictions, this characteristic set of interpretations will need to be checked. But what counts as evidence of 'correctness' for these meanings? The answer may be that 'correctness' comes from intersubjective agreement and this strongly recalls the previous arguments. But now we are talking in terms of personalities.

2

A Personal Construction of Personal Construct Theory

It was argued earlier that the adoption of a formalized personality theory would be a considerable advantage in the study of social relationships. Kelly's (1955, 1970) theory of personal constructs has been shown to have a basic position which reflects the main characteristics of the approach in the previous chapter, but its formal content remains to be inspected. Yet the basic position of 'constructive alterativism' (p. 14) leads Kelly to the elaboration of a formalized personality theory which reflects many more of the important emphases in Chapter 1.

Kelly uses the term 'constructs' for the categorizations, etc., which men devise and this shows one of the main overtones of the theory: man's personal responsibility for the (changing) tint of the spectacles through which he views the world. Although Personal Construct Theory is largely about *systems* of constructs, it is important to consider first what single constructs are. For example, by emphasizing the psychological nature (rather that the logical nature) of constructs, Kelly distinguishes between 'concepts' (with their overtones of 'real properties' residing in objects) and 'constructs' (which have overtones of imposed or attributed properties). In Kelly's view a construct takes its psychological meaning from the way it is used, since this serves to show not only which events the observer categorizes as similar but also to demonstrate which events he excludes. For psychologically (as opposed to logically) that which is implicitly denied is often as much a part of an individual's meaning in uttering a statement as what is explicitly affirmed, 'as when the disgruntled first mate entered in a ship's log that "the captain was sober tonight" ' (Kelly, 1969, p. 9).

Constructs thus operate as rules for classifying objects by discerning similarities between them and for distinguishing members of a class from some other classification by noting a contrast. Thus a construct does not just embrace a set of objects, people, events, etc., and *ignore* all others (as a logical concept does): rather it takes its *psychological* meaning from the fact that it embraces a set of objects and simultaneously offers exclusion of a property to other objects. For example, suppose I am presented with three people and told to classify them somehow. Two out of the three might by this method be classified as 'Scots'—the discerned similarity—and the third may be seen to be 'Irish'—the contrast. 'Scots–Irish' is thus a construct, but note how far the psychological meaning of the classification depends on the contrast. 'Scots–Irish' is clearly a distinction on crude grounds of nationality, but in the constructs 'Scots—Generous', 'Scots—Drinks beer', 'Scots—Plays the piano' some other psychological meaning is suggested, some other way of relating to the Scots. The two people (from my original three) in the class 'Scots' are still the same, but some other characteristic than a purely geographical one is suggested as part of my meaning. Again, the *psychological* meaning of 'Succeed–Fail' is clearly different from 'Succeed—Definitely *tries* to succeed', and the clarification of the sense of 'succeed' is provided by the contrast. Thus a construct is a basic contrast between two groups and it serves to distinguish between things and to group them. As such, constructs are reference axes against which objects may be referred and in terms of which the observer hopes to make sense of what he sees. Constructs are thus dichotomous items which embody a personal classification of events, etc., and a simultaneous contrast of this personal 'class' with another. This view provides the basis for a functional measurement of constructs which rests on the assessment of simultaneous similarity and contrast (see next section).

But there is more to a construct than a simple personal dichotomy, for constructs are essentially predictive, in Kelly's view. They are the ways in which predictions for the future are embodied in our psychological processes and represent expectancies of experience. Essentially, an individual construes by anticipating the ways in which past events will repeat themselves, and by induction he seeks to make his world predictable and manageable. However, events never repeat themselves exactly and the person must select those features which are, in his view, most appropriate and salient for the erection of a model wherewith to understand and be prepared for the future. All statements (and not just dispositional descriptions) thus assume, for Kelly, an element of tentative prediction. They are predictions because the speaker is selecting salient parts of the past in order to give himself a better understanding of the future; and they are tentative because the construer invites acceptance of a view which he may later wish to change for another in the light of further evidence. Such evidence may support or condemn his selection of 'salient parts of the past'. The inherent conceptual difficulties in grasping the implications of this stance are by no means eased by consideration of examples of constructs frequently given at this point in an exposition of Kelly's theory. Readers find constructs eloquently pronounced to be anticipatory, dichotomous affairs: elegant, complex, parts of our life, readily identifiable cogs of the machinery of everyday existence.

Then they read on and find constructs exemplified as 'black–white', 'two-stroke–four-stroke', 'Scots–Irish', etc. Truly, these may be constructs of a type at one level, but their patent failure to convey the exciting complexity of Kelly's notion is testimony to the fact that, if doubt exists, a consideration should be given to the discussions given by Kelly himself (Kelly, 1969).

On a similar point, it must be clear that these bare bones of the position necessarily omit the formal 'postulate' and 'corollary' structure in which the theory was presented (Kelly, 1955), but as thus far outlined, constructs are anticipatory, dichotomous and personal. They may also appear to be highly verbalized and dependent on language; yet Kelly rejected this charge with the claim that many unverbalized distinctions play a part in our activities. We often act on the basis of spontaneous aversions and infatuations for which we have no verbal description, and, for Kelly, these are constructs, too. While this may be so from the point of view which Kelly held, and for the purpose which he was completing, it is nevertheless the case that any outlook such as the present one which seeks to apply the theory must 'measure' constructs. In so doing it limits itself to consideration of those constructs which can be verbalized.

Just as single constructs are the personal components of an individual's psychological processes, so too the interconnections between constructs may be personal. The theory is as much about the connections within a system as it is about the individual constructs themselves. Each person is seen as erecting a system of constructs with which to represent and understand his experiences. Inevitably, constructs are associated with one another in personal ways, and PCT (Personal Construct Theory) is frequently concerned predominantly with the system which emerges. The typical lines of inference which characterize a system will dictate the meaning of constructs within that particular system (see Chapter 5). The whole system comprises an individual's personality and since the theory concerns both content and structure of systems, it offers a double line of inquiry. However, the structural investigation of an individual's semantic space has been most frequently selected for consideration (see Chapter 5), since it is associated with a useful method for operationalizing a person's interpretative outlook.

Links with the outlook in Chapter 1 become even clearer when one considers the metaphor on which Kelly alighted. In arranging his theory, Kelly had in mind the metaphor of 'man the scientist'. Man in general is seen to be as rational as a scientist in particular and similarly tries to understand the world and its constituent elements. By making this explicit, Kelly has provided the possibility of an account of the very processes which were considered in Chapter 1. The theory meets a requirement urged previously (p. 5) and accounts for man's propensity to hypothesize by making this the main object of its concern.

An implication of the position outlined above may, at first sight, suggest a limitation of the approach. For it is easy to feel that the emphasis on the *personal* nature of construing might commit us to solipsism and isolation. If we all speak private languages (it might be argued) then how do we deal with one another? But there are a couple of reasons why we are not liable to be entirely isolated by our own eccentric conceptual frameworks, unless the eccentricity begins to tend to be tinged with madness. The fact that absurdity can be produced within a system of constructs does not lead inevitably to the conclusion that all systems are irredeemably absurd; nor does the fact that unique constructs can be made lead to the corollary that personal construct systems are all unique and non-overlapping. However, the above objection may be posing the problem of *why* this is the case. Kelly devised a corollary in his theory which was specifically designed to describe the social process (see below, p. 24), but the above objection is at a different level and can be met differently. One answer is to suggest (Kelly, 1970, p. 3) that the limits of human ingenuity restrain the range of our alternative constructions. This confinement results in a good deal of similarity between individuals and so communication becomes possible. But this suggestion seems to run the risk of ignoring the many levels at which construing can occur and appears to propose that constructs are all of a type. However, although this may be so at some level, there is no reason to suppose that the same general statements are true of all of them: some construct-sharing may reflect feeble wits or timidity when we accept what is familiar or convenient, but at other levels, agreements may show something else. Another answer is to suggest that (far from being merely a result of limited ingenuity) our common acceptance of certain ways of construing reflects our reliance on one of the forms of social reality discussed earlier. Because we witness others using a construct in common with us we lack the evidence to suggest its possible insecurity. This clearly applies to several of the levels of social reality suggested above (p. 10), notably those concerned with language applicability or normative agreements. However, constructs may relate to all aspects of man's experience and need not concern just the normative and linguistic and objective levels. Constructs can be about opinions, or about other people's psychological characteristics—their habits, attitudes, styles, personalities—and individuals may seek to be relieved of any feeling of solipsism or isolation here, too. In short, they may seek to compare their constructs on these more contentious matters with the constructs of others in society. Thus a feature of the arguments of Chapter 1 is readily handled within the outlook of Kelly's theory and the arguments relating 'social processes' to specific social relationships can be phrased in the terms provided by this particular theory of personality.

Far from committing us to isolation or to a phenomenological insecurity, Kelly's theory offers us the means to understand communication with others and permits of links with the levels of social reality considered in Chapter

* *

1. It also has possibly fertile connections with the linguistic hypotheses of Whorf (1956) and Bernstein (1958). However, much of this facility is dependent on the methodology with which the theory is typically associated (see next section). Some of the value for this approach also depends on the relationship which the theory allows between 'personality' and yet other psychological concepts than those already considered. One main benefit rests with the theory's dynamic view of personality as a constant readjustment. It is this which couples with the emphasis on hypothesis and inquiry to give the theory its relevance to the central issues of the present position. However, it is also important that the theory allows a link between the concepts of 'attitude' and 'personality'. The constructs described above represent an individual's personal explanation of his situation to himself and are therefore the closest possible approximation to subjective attitudes on the minutiae of life. It could be argued that the phenomena treated as attitudes in the literature are simply constructs of a less fundamental nature, which represent the individual's way of ordering subjectively relevant and important information on topics which are somewhat arbitrarily chosen in the literature as being of greater importance and more indicative of some underlying pattern or process. Constructs are thus elements which are common to the two theoretical concepts: 'attitudes' and 'personality'. This crude differentiation will be elaborated and substantiated later when functional links between the two are clearer.

In view of the extensive critiques of Kelly's theory which are currently available (Bannister and Mair, 1968; Bannister, 1970; Bannister and Fransella, 1971) the present concern has been to identify those parts of his approach which direct the argument. The major importance of Kelly's research perspective here is in eschewing explanation in terms of drive-reduction, need-satisfaction or 'automatic' response to stimuli. The concern for understanding the individual in terms of his own verbalizations of his cognitive processes is tailor-made for the outlook adopted in Chapter 1. In measuring and revealing these verbalizations a specific method has been devised and has become an integral part of research which is based on the theory.

A METHODOLOGICAL TOOL

The Role Construct Repertory Test (Reptest) was devised by Kelly (1955) as a means of operationalizing construct measurement. Its essential aim was to allow an individual to produce his constructs in a form which could be clearly examined, so that his cognitive world could be understood *in his own terms*. The method admits of a way of determining not only the (idiosyncratic) content of an individual's constructs but also the (idiosyncratic) interrelations of constructs within the system. However, use of this test limits us to verbalizable constructs and its size determines the size of the sampling of the subject's total system. Its main advantage is that it is freely administered and does not channel the individual's answers by suggesting exact questions to him. This important methodological (and ideological) difference is considered empirically in Chapter 6.

In Kelly's view man is describing and at the same time selecting items from the past to use in his predictive structure. Since his categories and terms are potentially such personal constructions, the Reptest is a measure which differs from many others in order to tap an individual's semantic and psychological space. This method rests on Kelly's basic position and the further assumptions derived from it, that constructs (*not* objects, etc.) are best seen as dichotomous. Whatever an individual chooses to say about events, etc., takes its meaning from what contrasting things could also have been said relevantly. Thus constructs must be tapped as simultaneous similarities and contrasts.

But what aspects of his circumstances should the subject construe? In practice the experimenter usually focuses the subject on some particular items, such as photographs, other people, common situations, etc., depending on his requirements. The items which are to be construed are known as 'elements' and are considered in sets of three ('triads') according to a pattern predetermined by the experimenter. The subject's task is to differentiate among the three elements in each triad by finding a way in which two are similar and at the same time both different from the third (simultaneous similarity and contrast). For example, two may be 'smokers' and one a 'non-smoker'; or two may be 'kind' and the other 'unkind'; or two may 'Help me to learn things' while the third 'Makes things difficult for me'. Clearly the possible list of examples is virtually inexhaustible, since the experimenter is interested in *personal* meanings and those which characterize the individual. In order to make this process more efficient, the subject generates his own set of elements, within limits suggested by the experimenter. This usually ensures that the list is made up of people who are known to the subject personally. Furthermore, it is useful to ensure that all subjects have comparable (or even identical) ranges of elements in their list. To serve both of these requirements, all subjects are given a list of 'role titles' (i.e. names for roles that people perform, for example: mother, father, happy person) and they are asked to think of a different person for each role title. By making the element list include as wide a range as possible and by arranging for as many triads as possible to be construed, the experimenter is able to ensure that a wide sample of the subject's constructs is obtained. It is usual to instruct the subject not to repeat any of his constructs, as an additional means of extending the sampling range.

The resulting constructs are a sample of an individual's semantic space and, in Kelly's definition, part of his personality. The fact that the range is restricted and incomplete need not make the Reptest any worse or less satisfactory than any other personality test. Indeed, the Reptest's looser structuring has the advantage of allowing the individual to tell us in his own way how he views some of his circumstances. The question of the functional utility of this view of personality and its difference with other personality tests becomes an empirical question in Chapter 6. For the moment it is important to note that the evocation of a subject's own dimensions of discrimination presents us with some parts of his own everyday cognitions. It makes it possible to relate 'personality' to everyday life and this in turn facilitates the view that friendship formation and everyday behaviour are closely related (as argued in Chapter 1). It is thus possible to eschew explanations of friendship in terms which have been specially imported for that topic alone.

IMPLICATIONS FOR INTERPERSONAL ATTRACTION

The fertility of PCT as a theory and a methodology has been shown in many areas (Bannister and Fransella, 1971), but the application of it to the area of friendship formation and interpersonal attraction has previously been less than fully clarified. Yet it has immense fertility here also. In raising this discussion one is not attempting to decide whether PCT was really a friendship theory all along, nor to argue that Kelly was *really* on about acquaintance and the social process. Such disputations would have the same value as deciding whether the theory is Zen Buddhist or Existentialist or whatever else it is often claimed to be. Kelly rightly rejected the claims of the persistent labellers who settled on the theory: not because he was not an Existentialist or a Zen Buddhist, etc; nor because he could not see similarities between his theory and those others. These were not the grounds of his rejection of such claims. His grounds appear to be that such labels tell us little *about* the theory (and especially they tell us very little about the particular implications of the theory). The value of the theory does not lie in its similarity to other outlooks, for encyclopaedic categorization merely obscures and detracts from detailed study of the theory's individual qualities and potential. Apart from its perceptive claim that people construe things (such as theories) in different ways, its value lies in the challenge which the theory offers for those who wish to examine its fertility for new areas. So Kelly's theory is an important cornerstone in this argument not only because it centres on man's established and pervasive propensity for hypothesis and interpretation; nor solely because it presents a formalized elaboration of some concepts central to the standpoint of Chapter 1. Nor even is it because the theory contains the means to address the problem of interpersonal attraction from within its formal structure (see below). The main advantage for the current outlook is the extent of the possibilities which its perspective offers in the area of social relationships.

Kelly's view is that man's normal processes are based on an inclination to 'understand' and he incorporates this emphasis on subjective explanation into the formal framework of his theory of personality. It was claimed earlier that a personality theory was an essential component of a coherent approach to interpersonal relationships and this personality theory, by its emphasis on interpretation, represents many of the proposals of Chapter 1. It thus formally allows of links between 'personality' and the area of 'interpersonal attraction'. This kind of view can be facilitated by suggesting that evidence is provided for the value of one's own constructs by comparison with the constructs of others. Social reality for constructs can be gained by associating with others; social reality for constructs of particular kinds (e.g. those relating to the psychological characteristics of others) can be provided by associating with particular others. Thus the adoption of this particular theory of personality (with its unique formalization of the nature of the elements of a personality) allows us to represent the subtlety of the levels at which social comparison occurs. This can be done by understanding the process of attraction in terms of comparison of constructs.

However, it was claimed above that our understanding of attraction processes may be aided by consideration of some parts of the internal structure of PCT itself. Is there any rationale provided by the corollaries of PCT which would combine intrinsic justification for the present view with the extrinsic values and usefulness pointed out above? Although the full extent of PCT's formal structure has not yet been displayed here, recourse may be had to two of the corollaries in this instance.

Because of the particular and special peculiarities of each individual's use of constructs and the structuring of their implications and interconnections, no two adult individuals can ever be exactly the same in cognitive structure. Nevertheless, as argued above, some overlap is both necessary and certain in order to avoid complete isolation and solipsism. Kelly's original exposition (Kelly, 1955) included two corollaries which can be interpreted as helping here. The *commonality corollary* states that 'To the extent that one person employs a construction of experience which is similar to that employed by another, his processes are psychologically similar to those of the other person'. He does not argue that similar individuals will have had similar experiences, but that they will have similar construction processes. Thus, in Kelly's terms, similarity of construct systems amounts to similarity of personality. The other corollary which helps here is the *sociality corollary*. This states that 'To the extent that one person construes the construction processes of another he may play a role in social processes involving the other person'. Thus the extent of our intelligible and productive relations with another is limited by the extent to which we understand what he is up to. The definition of our involvement, if you like, rests on our comprehension of why the other person does what he does. The corollary is saying that it is not enough merely to construe another's *behaviour* in this context: it is necessary to construe his construction processes (Kelly, 1970), to have some grasp of the rules by which he is operating, or some conception of what he thinks is happening. But the corollary is not saying our construction must be correct (see also Chapter 12).

Presumably it follows from these two corollaries that commonality of processes is conducive to an increase in the possibilities for construing another's processes and thus enhances the likelihood of social communication. However, it is an important point that mere knowledge of another's processes is not sufficient for the type of social process envisaged in this programme. One can know the constructs of a child or a despised antagonist without friendship being an inevitable outcome. Knowledge of another's processes does not necessarily imply similarity of one's processes to his, and so the type of 'social process' which constitutes friendship is a much more developed and specific type of process than that covered here by Kelly and it requires the blending of these two corollaries to provide a theoretical basis within the Kellian framework.

Development of this point implies that the more one finds particular similarities with another particular person, the greater will be the understanding of his processes (because they are similar to one's own) and therefore the greater the ability to communicate in a comprehensible world. It is therefore derivable from within the structure of PCT that similarity of construing processes will facilitate the formation of friendships. Insofar as Kelly deals with this problem, then, his view would predict that friendship follows from similarity of construing processes because it eases communication.

However, a stronger view is also possible here and derives its force from a consideration of the *functional* utility of similarity. It may clearly be extended to subsume construct similarity. Kelly supposed that individuals erect not only construct systems but also several kinds of subjective criteria with which to judge their applicability and validity. Constructs are themselves measured against the individual's view of the evidence and are discarded or changed if they appear to be mistaken, inadequate or incomplete. Events can thus be reconstrued within a partly altered framework and it was the process of modification of the system as a function of experience which Kelly saw as the main force behind man's behaviour. In this way, constructs are validated and invalidated as predictions by being compared with the way in which events apparently unfold. Any apparent circularity which this suggests can be seen to rest with the individual: he makes the predictions; he decides if they were right. However, it is surely a much stronger method of validation to find one's constructs *shared* and this must count subjectively as evidence for their merit, just as it may do to find that they meet other subjectively erected criteria for success. The more constructs one shares with others the more the constructs will seem to be well formed and justified. Similarity is, on this account, not just something incidentally beguiling for an individual but is something functionally important. It provides a measure of social reality, cements his subjective interpretations and categorizations of that which is outside and reinforces his subjective structuring of experience. Thus the value of construct similarity becomes clearer, and more clearly linked with the 'social reality' suggested by Festinger (1954).

This latter view is based also on that of Byrne (1961) and is discussed in Chapter 4. However, both this suggestion and the 'similarity aids communication' claim are derivable from the theory of personal constructs and serve to direct the course of this investigation.

3

Studying Interpersonal Attraction

In order to discuss certain of the phenomena which surround us, it is often convenient to arrange them into more or less arbitrary groupings or classes so that the process of thinking and talking about them is made easier. This much was argued in Chapter 1, but applies no less to the activities of psychologists than to those of Everyman. The point is that such 'everyday' methods have implications for psychological study and description, too. For it is all too easy to separate 'areas' of psychology and to reify labels in just the ways mentioned in Chapter 1. In so doing, one may too readily lose sight of relationships between areas.

Awareness of this possibility is of great assistance in the discussion of interpersonal relationships and the 'area' of interpersonal attraction, since it highlights certain pitfalls and it is crucial to the theoretical development envisaged here. While the uses of such arbitrary classifications of phenomena are as readily apparent here as they were for 'normal man' on pages 8–9 (ease of communication, order, convenience, etc.), there are also some clear disadvantages, for it tends to suggest two (possibly misleading) inferences. It is useful at this stage to point them out and to elaborate their effects. One is the inference that, in some indefinite way, the area is a neat compartment of man's behavioural repertoire which can be studied in relative isolation. This is an example of the fallacy of naming and labelling, which suggests (to a user of a subject–predicate-based language) that we have actually identified a fact of nature, which merely waved its name clearly and explicitly before our eyes. The second misleading consequence is that there is created a false appearance of compact unity and uniformity within the bounds of the 'area'.

Naturally, there is a sense in which it is useful to assume that areas represent parts of behaviour which can fruitfully be regarded as separate processes, but one must ever temper this with the caution that its main benefit derives from the convenience of 'shorthand thinking'. It may be very convenient at one level to talk in terms of 'social man' as distinct from, say, 'instinctive man', while yet recognizing at another level the oversimplification which this embodies. But just as the professional psychologist is not to be deprived of his membership of the class of human beings just because he studies (or is, at this very moment, studying) particular types of problem, so also is it equally undesirable to divorce man's processes in particular situations (e.g. forming friendships, conforming, showing helping behaviour) from his processes as a whole. This is not, of course, to deny that there may be shifts of *emphasis*, but it disclaims differences in process.

It is true that in the area marked 'interpersonal attraction' man can be seen as following an essentially different course from that followed in the area labelled 'conformity', but he does not therefore renounce his usual range of cognitive activities any more than he repudiates his humanity. Even when he is forming friendships, the individual may still conform or be altruistic, since the activities are not mutually exclusive. If his normal behaviour constitutes evaluation and hypothesis, then his perception of other persons may contain elements of this, too. In making relative evaluations of others, the individual may consult all manner of cues (see Chapter 4). Indeed at some level of early acquaintance there may be no difference at all between person perception and friendship formation, since exactly the same processes may serve two functions at this time. In view of this possibility, it would be shortsighted to restrict ourselves to the 'area' of interpersonal attraction.

The second misleading impression created by a single area label was identified earlier as that of a uniformity in the phenomenon studied. This point bears on the previous one, as may be clear, for it is necessary to identify some similarity in particular phenomena which separates them from the general mass of phenomena before they can be treated as an area. But by continuing to concentrate on the similarities between the members of a class and applying a uniform explanation to all of them, the appearance of unity is unduly emphasized and much that is peculiar is inevitably lost. For example, it may be erroneous to assume that attraction to strangers, cross-sex and same-sex choices, friendship in children, etc., are all governed entirely by the same principles at the molecular level, simply because the 'area' of interpersonal attraction subsumes them all. Later on, the sense in which it is erroneous will become clearer, as will the sense in which it is not. At another level of example, but on a related point, it would clearly be simple-minded to apply even specific hypotheses to the area in too uniform and undifferentiating a manner. Consider how, otherwise, one may have to treat the venerable saw 'Birds of a feather flock together'. While this may be seen to suggest that similarity is an attractive principle, it does not mean that the similarity would be total. It does not imply that friendship pairs involving person A would characteristically show similarity of the same aspects of personality, such that all his friends had the appearance of psychological Siamese twins. One must expect different sides of natures to be shown in different friendships, as might follow from reflection on Kelly's explanation of social processes (Chapter 2) in terms of one's understanding of the other person involved.

It is also easy to compound functional confusion between 'attraction' and 'friendship', if one relies too incautiously on the convenience of regarding interpersonal attraction as an 'area'. The model elaborated in the next chapter rests squarely on the distinction between these two levels of acquaintance. But the confusion is another example of the results of a process which is convenient at one level but misleading at another. Although classification indubitably provides a useful guide, it must not be allowed to obscure the realization that the arbitrariness of classes means that events, phenomena, etc., cannot only be included in a class but can be seen simultaneously to be members of more than one class. Just as *pyrus malus* can be an example of 'edible objects', so might some of the phenomena of 'friendship formation' be examples of 'person perception' and vice versa. Therefore it is important to bear in mind that any number of events which is arbitrarily assembled and branded as 'interpersonal attraction' is an arbitrary assembly, and the brand is not indelible. Similarly, such an assembly of events is not thenceforward an island unto itself but continues to be an assembly of events, etc., taken from the overall assembly which has been labelled 'Behaviour (human)'.

These problems and difficulties are brought to the fore when considering how to represent the 'area' in a way which renders its study possible and useful. It is necessary to simplify the complexities by some means and 'areas' are a first step. This imposition of order can make the problems more specific and manageable, but the danger remains that one fails to distinguish the baby from the bath water, for one is never quite sure of what has been eliminated in the process of making the problem a tractable one for experimental examination. However, this type of simplification is a different type from that exemplified in naiveté, in that recognition of the complexities is a pre-requisite, not merely a consequence of investigation.

SOME BASIC PROBLEMS

It is the very complexity of the topic which is the source of many of the problems here. It will be seen that in most cases the problems are a result of the conflict between 'nature' (which is complex) and 'science' (whose rigorous requirements appear to necessitate that phenomena are reduced for examination).

Of course, there are many levels at which this simplification can be devised. One has already been mentioned (breaking down into 'areas'). A further kind of simplification requires that (to begin with, at least) only some parts of an isolated 'area' should be considered. Paradigmatic instances are identified and given close attention until the store of accumulated knowledge justifies extension to further paradigms. Thus, while it is obvious that there are many kinds of 'friendship' and 'attraction' (same-sex, cross-sex, bosom pals, attraction to new acquaintances, established friendships, marital selections, etc.), empirical slimming dictates that some kinds must initially be treated as less centrally relevant. For example, those who meet solely on the occasions when they play bridge or operate aircraft may 'get on well' with one another. Yet if they meet only for those purposes and on those occasions, then they are (at present, anyway) of less interest than those cases where the participants meet each other for their own sakes, even if they also play bridge or operate aircraft. In studying interpersonal attraction one is interested not in attraction to group *qua* group (where the individual constituent members are less important than is the function of the group), but where individuals are attracted to others as individuals.

Even when such simplification and narrowing of the topic has been effected, the pivotal questions still remain. Why does social intercourse occur? Why are particular selections made among the range of all those who are ever encountered? These two questions have often been taken independently of one another: Schachter (1959) studied the problem of what tended to increase the affiliative need, in the general case; Byrne (1961) addressed himself to the problem of particular selections; other examples are given in the next chapter. However, the argument so far expounded enables us to combine explanation of the two questions. Social reality at all manner of levels is provided by social intercourse and particular selections reflect the search for particular kinds of social reality testing.

The further questions might begin with the characterization of the development of friendship. Are there changes in kind or merely of degree? As an extension and particularization of this, can we suggest a basis for the observation that reunions of erstwhile bosom pals are so frequently characterized by boredom, embarrassment and intense urges to leave? A dynamic theory of personality (such as that discussed in Chapter 2) might offer an explanation in terms of cognitive changes on a time scale. Whatever explanation is attempted, it is clear that any theory must tackle the decay and deterioration of established friendships just as much as it requires access to an explanation of how they become established.

A further desideratum is the prediction of eventual friendships on the basis of information available after only a few encounters. Not only would such omniscience yield commercial fruit (witness 'computer dating') but would also have serious heuristic value for personnel selection, marriage counselling and many other areas (see Chapter 12). Such considerations reiterate the need to see this area as rooted in normal processes. Its relation to other parts of man's behaviour is a constantly reverberating theme here and is no less important than its relation to personality. The view that evaluation and hypothesis characterize our interpersonal relations has several further implications. For example, it leaves us holding the responsibility for our relationships, since it eschews a rigid 'A *causes* B' paradigm with its overtones of inevitability, determinism and its tacit denial of the effects of the substitution of persons. On our view, the person's view of the situation renders its effects relative. A further implication involves a reversal of the women's magazine approach. In this latter kind of view, people carry round templates of (say) Mr. Right. This suggests that friendships result from the fulfilment of certain criteria. The present proposal will espouse the view that friendships result from the failure to present negatively evaluated data and the marriage of this criterion with the disclosure of psychological similarity. This, of course, suggests that *all* social encounters are potential friendship situations unless something debars their fruition.

PRACTICAL PROBLEMS

Of course, a recognition of some of the problems and aims of the study of interpersonal attraction does not necessarily promote their solution. Given the prevailing contemporary emphasis on 'scientific rigour', one must set about the isolation of the factors involved in friendship formation and the control of extraneous variables. Before consideration is directed to the factors which have been advocated (Chapter 4), it makes sense to review the general implications of this requirement and the methods which have been adopted in its fulfilment.

One necessary condition is that the topic must be reduced and studied where it comes out into the open, even if it is normally embedded in real life. All this is a familiar part of the social scientific enterprise, but such study has its pitfalls and alertness to the dangers may be illuminating. When returning from an empirical safari, it is as well to remind one's theoretical self of what may have been left behind at the start. Thus, while bowing for the moment to the requirements of scientific study, one may wish later to exercise an option for the return to holism.

Studies on aspects of interpersonal attraction are particularly prone to a common charge against psychological investigation. It is frequently argued that one difference between social and natural science is the reactive effects of study: that is to say, the act of being studied causes unrepresentative behaviour to be shown. Truly, copper sulphate crystals do not suddenly change when taken into the laboratory. For example, they do not become anxious or suspicious, so far as we know. Human subjects, it is claimed, often do suffer such change. The 'artificiality' of the laboratory situation alters their behaviour so that it is unrepresentative; and we are often warned of the dangers. This may present especial difficulties for the area of friendship formation. The artificiality of sitting people down to form friendships need not be dwelt on.

However, it will be noticed that two points may be confused here. It is one thing to claim that laboratory study upsets normal behaviours; it is quite another to claim that laboratory studies are artificial (i.e. unreal, unrepresentative of that which they seek to examine). So the attentive are again rewarded: if we assume that man's normal ventures involve inquiry, suspicion, hypothesis and test, then there is no essential difference from normal behaviour portrayed if he exemplifies such behaviour in the laboratory; secondly, if one studies friendship formation on a basis which is not purely experimental (i.e. involves a reliance on measurement rather than manipulation) the situation retains the flavour of reality and the subject's suspicions can have less appreciable distorting influences on the information gathered. Use of the Reptest would offer further assistance since it is not possible to 'lie' when completing the test.

However, in this area laboratory study runs the additional risk of superficiality to quite a large extent. The use of (say) seven-point scales (from 1: 'Dislike' to 7: 'Like very much') as measures of attraction carries its own inherent problems, for surely we would find it hard enough to distinguish our established relationships on such scales (what does a rating of 5 *mean*?), but if confronted with the task of rating a stranger, then how can we proceed sensibly? How can the scale be grounded when comparison ratings of known friends are not included? Thus, when confronted with the problem of operationalizing friendship, the present studies (except one, where the paradigm of other investigators was adopted) all allowed subjects to define friendship for themselves and merely requested that they should 'name their friends' (see method sections in subsequent chapters). A check on the reality of this procedure was enshrined in the reliance on *mutual* choices from these free lists as the functional criterion of friendship. It is possible to obtain graphic records of friendship choices for consultation, using the methods of sociometry. Table 3.1 exemplifies the graphic results of such techniques and illustrates data actually collected in Experiment B (Chapter 6). These methods were adopted in most of the studies reported here.

Once such problems of reduction and operationalization have been handled (although one could not claim to have solved them) one can look to possible methods of dealing with the material one has allowed for consideration. Details of analytical procedures are given in subsequent chapters, but it is illuminating to examine the broad outlines of research techniques which are available here. It is possible to identify two fundamentally different approaches (which are not incompatible): the 'experimental'

Table 3.1. An example of the sociometric choice matrices used during the analysis of most of the experiments reported in these studies. These data are actually from Experiment B (a cross represents a mutual choice; a stroke represents an unreciprocated choice)

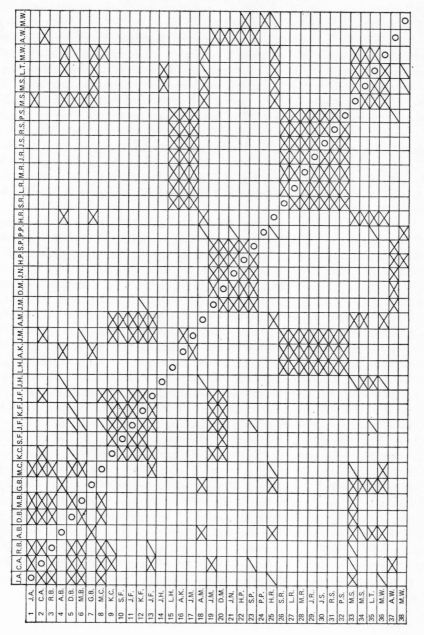

approach and the 'correlational' approach. In experimental studies, some factor (independent variable) is manipulated experimentally and a study is made of the effect which this has on some other factor (dependent variable). Thus, for example, one might vary levels of payment (independent variable) and study the effects of this on work output (dependent variable). Or one might manipulate levels of attitude similarity (independent variable) and measure the resulting levels of attraction (dependent variable). However, in this area such methods run into problems of the representativeness of the experimental situation. (Is it usual to be presented with an attitude scale completed by another person? Do the attitudes on attitude scales reflect the values discussed in real life? Is direct access to a person's data functionally the same as the access one has in social intercourse? Note the difference here between concern with attitudes on a scale and concern with the subject's own way of expressing himself as revealed by his constructs). Such problems may also reflect the difficulty of indulging the subject's credibility in the manipulations.

Some of these difficulties may be avoided (at the expense of incurring others) by adopting a different method. The correlational method is essentially one which measures two (or more) aspects of the world without any manipulation other than that involved in the original discovery of two samples with different characteristics. The relationship between the two variables is then the source of interest. Thus one might find a set of highly paid workers and see if their work output is also high. Or one might find a group of friends and give them tests which would disclose whether they evidence similarity on one dimension or another. In practice, an amalgam of these two paradigms is usually employed since the correlational method in its purest form is afflicted with the difficulty that it demonstrates association (A goes with B) but gives no indication of the direction of causality (Does A cause B or does B cause A?). However, if 'experimental' techniques risk artificiality, 'correlational' techniques may be able to offer a truer picture of real life. Indeed, some experimental investigators are all too aware of the possible artificiality of their methods and are at pains to evade the criticism. Occasionally it is confronted directly, by the completion of 'continuity studies' (e.g. Byrne, Ervin and Lamberth, 1970, who studied the links between experimental studies of attraction and 'real-life computer dating'—see Chapter 4, for a discussion of this experiment). Such studies facilitate the conclusion that one has not entirely lost sight of the original problem by reducing it for study. (N.B. Studies of continuity between 'life' and 'laboratory' are of course a different brand from those which claim the continuity of the effects of a given factor at several levels of acquaintance—for example, Berscheid, Dion, Walster and Walster, 1971; cf., Chapters 11 and 12 below.)

Investigators handle these problems in several different ways and have offered several kinds of explanation for the topics of our common interest. Despite the fact that so large a number of problems face this area, the literature on friendship and attraction is a testament to psychologists' dogged obstinacy in the face of opposition! The next chapter investigates the theoretical and empirical approaches to the area and spells out a theory for study here.

4

The Problems of Interpersonal Attraction

Within the 'area' which is frequently described as 'the attraction literature' or 'interpersonal attraction' there are three broad categories of phenomena investigated: attraction to strangers who have never been met; attraction to people who have been met for a brief period of interaction at some basal level; and various forms of 'cohesiveness'. The distinction between the first two and the latter category is one based on the depth of acquaintance of those concerned, and 'cohesiveness' here includes naturally occurring friendship groups (Izard, 1960, 1963), group cohesion studies (Lott and Lott, 1965), and choice of marital partners (Walster, Aronson, Abrahams and Rottman, 1966). Studies of dating or of *prediction* of marital choice, etc. (e.g. Byrne, Ervin and Lamberth, 1970) are largely studies in the first two categories. By and large, it can be seen that the first two broad categories correspond to the experimental paradigm and the latter category perforce exemplifies the correlational paradigm—a functional and methodological distinction just outlined in Chapter 3.

While the methodological differences are frequently pointed out (e.g. Byrne, Ervin and Lamberth, 1970), the conceptual distinctions between the objects of studies in the different categories are often blurred and the speculation is often expressed that links between 'attraction to strangers' and 'choice of marital partners' (for example) *may* be found (Byrne et al., 1970). Even where any distinction is made (e.g. Senn, 1971) it is not always clear that researchers in one area regard themselves as investigating a phenomenon which differs essentially from the other two.

Only very recently has it begun to be asserted that the factors which determine attraction may be different from those which determine prolonged friendship (Hogan and Mankin, 1970; Lischeron and La Gaipa, 1970; Duck and Spencer, 1972), but this has merely served to point out that satisfactory explanations for this suggestion are currently in short supply. Indeed it will be argued below that such possibilities enmesh in difficulty many of the presented attraction theories (e.g. Winch, 1958; Walster, 1965; Byrne, 1969). It may be that such difficulties do not present themselves to a view which adopts a subjectivist, rather than a determinant, stance.

The arguments to be presented in this chapter will view the conceptual distinctions between:

(a) Mere acquaintance (i.e. the mere encounter of another);
(b) Attraction to strangers who have not been met in the flesh before or during experiments on attraction (and, especially, the evidence about them which is supposed to generate the attraction), for example, subjects are sometimes presented with the attitude scale of 'another subject', whom they have not seen.
(c) Attraction to those who have been met briefly;
(d) Friendship (at its many levels—the levels of interest here will primarily be those where affinity is independently and functionally assessable); and
(e) Choice of marital partners;

as essential to any understanding of an overall 'Acquaintance Process' (Newcomb, 1961)—from 'mere encounter' to any of the levels of friendship —since the distinctions as laid out above provide for a *logical* progression from passing acquaintance to firm friendship. For convenience, it will often be useful to talk in terms of 'stages', but this is another useful shorthand with hidden dangers, for it may suggest the claim that hard-and-fast sequential categories will be delineated. This is an optimistic claim, at the very best, and, given the profound complexity of the process of acquaintance, the safest proposal is that certain emphases predominate from time to time, certain parts of the process assume a greater importance as a function of the development of acquaintance, a certain ebb and flow of the relative weights of different activities takes place. In this complex situation, it clearly makes some sense, therefore, to refer to the *process* in terms of these supposed fluxes and transient predominances, and these, for convenience, may be seen as 'stages'.

Implicit in this view is the repudiation of any notion that 'mere acquaintance' and 'friendship' are the book-ends of the process, with every other stage serving as a transition between the two (with an implication of 'goals', 'ends', etc.). It is unlikely that all new acquaintances are scrutinized with the specific *intention* of considering them for friends, although this may indeed happen occasionally. For while some people may set out to choose and deliberately make particular others into friends, a more un-reasoned, unconscious and universal process is felt to be the main one. Equally, previous argument rejects any kind of formal determinism in the type of explanation offered (i.e. no adoption of the view that A necessarily implies B), for it will be seen from the previous chapters that great emphasis is placed here on subjective *evaluation* of such factors; on the *infirmity* of such rigid classifications as the above implies; on the inclusion of 'specific parts' of man's behavioural repertoire in the *context* of his general processes;

and on the *sense in which* it is safe to regard 'the acquaintance process' as separable and unique.

The particular positive suggestion of this viewpoint is that the Acquaintance Process can usefully be regarded as a parallel to the logical progression indicated above and may be seen in terms of the operation of 'filters' by means of which individuals select from the total population those who can be considered potential friends, and how they select out by continual reduction a low number of people whom they regard as close friends. 'The operation of filters' can be seen to be an intentionally ambiguous phrase, in that 'operation' may be both transitive and intransitive ('he operates the filters'; 'the filters operate'), and this retains the ambiguity of whether filters are conscious, unconscious or a partial integration of each.

It may be clear at this stage that this filtering theory, while sharing more than a commonality of terms with that of Broadbent (1964), is yet distinct from the latter. In Broadbent's terms, filtering is the selective reduction in information-handling capacity which is a necessary and inevitable concomitant of a system with a finite number of parts. In the terms of the present theory, filtering is the selective reduction of the number of persons still regarded as potential friends as a result of subjective evaluation of the cues which these potential friends appear to manifest.

To elucidate the propositions of this present theory of filtering, it is necessary to consider the types of 'group' which have been studied in the literature; the type of findings which have been reported; the theories which have been suggested, and the types of question and shortcomings which have been revealed. For it may be that those things which present a fertile ground for continuing friendships are not those which originally precipitate it, although they were present even at the start. They may, in other words, be necessary factors but not sufficient ones, and a theory which replaces 'causal factors' and 'determinants' with a notion of 'selective filters' dependent on subjective explanation and interpretation could show how such is the case.

THE ACQUAINTANCE PROCESS

The formation of particular friendships occurs perforce within the range of others encountered by an individual and the central question (see Chapter 1) is plainly why he chooses *particular* others from the general mass of possibilities. The character of the aggregate in which he is seen to be contained will doubtless contribute substantially to his choice behaviour, and it is at this level that the first type of filter can be seen to operate.

It is possible to see the reflection of the 'historical' development of the acquaintance process in the historical development of studies into it. Early work directed its attention to 'situationally induced' groups and found that one important influence in determining an individual's choices was proximity (Festinger, Schachter and Back, 1950). In other words, friendship groups were often composed of next-door neighbours; and Homans (1950) and Gullahorn (1952) similarly suggested that frequency of interaction played a part in friendship formation—a finding which has been extended by Darley and Berscheid (1967) who show that expectation of interacting with another has an important effect on attraction levels.

However, such things are treated as factors which cause, determine, effect (rather than affect) friendship, but this is so only in a restricted sense, for if an individual never meets or interacts with someone (in the widest sense, to include communication by letter or telephone, for example), or expects never to see them later, then there is little ground for friendship formation. In the latter case, inhibition of (or simple failure to continue) any processes of evaluation may result in the discarding of the person from the pool of those regarded as potential friends. In Chapter 3 it was suggested that some inhibiting factor was a hindrance to friendship, rather than that something positive, some *determinant* was necessarily present to *cause* friendship. So, clearly, the above are examples of 'factors' like this, which are necessary but *not* sufficient for friendship formation. Empirical evidence for this suggestion is found in Warr (1965), where it is shown that proximity of this type was a determinant of both positive and negative sociometric choices. In other words, proximity does not guarantee positive feelings and some other concepts are required. Such situational factors are better taken as having a filtering effect, in subdividing the total pool of people who are encountered into those who can usefully be regarded as potential friends and those who cannot. But the central question still remains.

When such an aggregate has occurred adventitiously and individuals brought together as a result of situational factors have begun to interact, then such things as physical attractiveness and personal attributes can begin to play a part in the interaction and may present the actors with cues on which selections can be based in the acquaintance process. It has been suggested (Berscheid, Dion, Walster and Walster, 1971) that physical attractiveness acts as a 'gatekeeper' for interaction with members of the opposite sex, and while no systematic attempt is made there to introduce any general notion akin to 'filtering', the idea is not inconsistent with it. Indeed, the fact that physical characteristics and attractiveness serve a filtering function for individuals in the selection of friends of *both* sexes, is a natural extension of previous findings at this level (Byrne, London and Reeves, 1968) and merely requires the additional hypothesis that individuals make evaluations of certain types of characteristic. Stroebe, Insko, Thompson and Layton (1971) have presented results which suggest further ways in which physical attractiveness can operate to serve a filtering function. They found that physical attractiveness was a factor in *dating* choice, but not in selection of marital partners. This suggests first that there are characteristically different stages of attraction; second, that at different stages of attraction, different types of cue are attended to; and third, that cues may lose their force as the acquaintance develops. The results thus give further evidence that situations and physical characteristics are not cues-for-all, but are interpreted according to subjects' cognitions and, it seems, intentions.

Nor need one assume that it is only physical characteristics which can be thus treated and interpreted, for the literature is full of examples of cues which have been found to be connoted evaluatively (e.g. spectacles—Thornton, 1944; lipstick—McKeachie, 1952; clothes—Flugel, 1950; racial characteristics—Razran, 1950).

Such processes operate in a very gross way, since one single cue of the above type is, at best, unreliable evidence at this stage for the types of generalization which are sometimes produced by subjects in experiments (Asch, 1946; Warr and Knapper, 1968). The more information one has organized about someone from perception, the less one will need to fabricate information 'supplied' by one's own cognitive structure and stereotypes, the more secure is any evaluation of him; and the information can be increased by face-to-face interaction. Argyle and McHenry (1971) found that spectacles influenced subjects' ratings of intelligence only when presented as a variable in still photographs, but lost any such effect when presented as a variable in videotapes of 5-minute interviews. The cues which have been isolated in studies of interaction are numerous (Argyle, 1970), but here again, results can be re-interpreted to fall in with a theory of filter processing. Burns (1964) showed that such unconscious pieces of behaviour as the distance at which individuals stand from those with whom they interact, affects the impressions formed by others and one can argue that the impressions depend on the way in which others interpret and evaluate the act. Davitz (1964) reports that the same message read in different tones of voice can create different impressions for observers, and Mehrabian (1971) has shown the subtle differences in language which can convey to a listener different impressions of a speaker's attitudes; for example, differences in 'immediacy' (the degree of directness or intensity of interaction between the speaker and the object which he speaks about) can be conveyed in subtle linguistic ways (e.g. these–those; here–there; Du–Sie; 'himself' as used by the Irish; ille–iste in Latin: these all point to the universality of the phenomenon—Brown, 1965). Judgements about an individual's feelings towards objects or people may be affected by perception and evaluation of such differences. Several general impressions (e.g. sincerity, friendliness, involvement) can be created by such simple cues in interaction and this invites the proposition that attention (perhaps unconscious attention) to such cues could be a variable in the filtering process.

Such findings have most usually been associated with the area of person perception, but the links between person perception and other processes claimed in Chapter 1 may now be more apparent. The contention here is that the processes described in person perception studies have such close links with those involved in the 'area' of attraction and friendship formation (amongst others), that one begins to want to ask whether they are conceptually distinct at all. So much may be clear up to now, where concern has so far centred on the types of cue which have interested the workers on person perception. Later it will be argued that all these perceptual activities have a specific function and provide 'evaluative evidence' about personality at a time when 'direct evidence' is not available. However, before doing so it is necessary to elaborate the directions which the acquaintance process takes now; the cues which may then come into focus; and the functions which these may serve. It is then necessary to consider some of the theories which account for friendship in terms of cognitive processes and to evaluate their approaches.

THE NATURE OF THE PROGRESSIVE DEVELOPMENT OF FRIENDSHIP

The argument so far in this chapter has been that the interpretation of simple cues, the organization of these interpretations and subsequent evaluations of their origin, is the process (if it is a single process) which, in real life, can be taken to be that which begins to distinguish realized friendship from the merely potential. The cues have so far been those things which are indisputably 'there' (spectacles, clothes, etc.) and variation is accountable to the different evaluations made of them. The link between this and the types of comment made in Chapter 1 may now be clearer, for these are the types of cue which correspond most nearly to the kinds of dimensions measured by rulers and hydrometers. In Chapter 1 the discussion then turned to a discussion of factors which were not 'there' in the same sense: namely to individual personality characteristics, 'motivation', etc. In parallel with this, any consideration of the development of friendship must shift now to a discussion of more complex and less 'factual' cues. Those things which have been discussed as cues for filtering so far are, by and large, those things which are outside the 'owner's' control, while face-to-face interaction increasingly introduces those types of cue from an individual which require to be understood in terms of his personal interpretative system. At the very lowest level, factors mediating (or filters involved in the selection process during) early acquaintance are those which are to some extent imposed from outside on individuals, or involve also, to some extent, unconscious processes. Situational and 'ecological' factors (place of living, physical position in a factory set-up, those you meet in your 'usual' compartment on the commuter train, etc.) are typical instances of how the range of acquaintances might be restricted in this way. But later there is a dove-tailing of this type of filter with others of a more refined and subtle nature, until a conscious process of evaluation, interpretation and subjective explanation begins to push forward.

At the same time, the type of cue considered is the subject of a similar 'upward shift' from the physical characteristics to those immediately concerned with more cognitive attributes. There are no clear black-and-white cut-off points suggested here as will be clear from some of the previous discussion. What is envisaged are minute shifts of emphasis, nevertheless conjoined at times with obvious and sudden changes of the focus of attention. Hoffman (1958) and Hoffman and Maier (1966) have argued on similar lines that situational factors place limits on and can frequently completely overwhelm consideration of other characteristics by individuals. By making the additional distinctions between 'friendship levels' and between the necessary and sufficient conditions for friendship, the present theory can weave this suggestion into a wider fabric, for it assists an understanding of the changes which are being considered here.

Underlying the shifts of emphasis in filtering, and inextricably part of the nexus of processes involved, lies the process which is taken by this viewpoint to be the central aim of individuals selecting those with whom friendship assumes a positive lustre. For after the operation of the earlier filtering—the main situational and simple evaluative components—the individuals are here hypothesized to make two shifts. One is to concern themselves with ways of describing the other's personality and personal characteristics; the other is to evaluate the personality so described for some type of overlap with their own. The implications of descriptive methods and the types of 'overlap' now become the main concern for this argument.

It is, for example, an empirical question whether individuals use particular types of description to characterize their better-known acquaintances and friends, and this question will be tackled later (Chapters 8–9). Furthermore, evidence will be presented in Chapter 9 that the description of another's personality is the aim and ultimate purpose of all the earlier and lower-level description and evaluation which may characterize interactions. However, the implications of the function which this may serve are largely theoretical questions and there is no lack of views to explain the types of overlap which may be sought. The word 'overlap' is deliberately chosen as an ambiguous 'class title' for this reason. For explanations have separately been offered in terms of reciprocity-of-liking, 'matching', complementarity and similarity.

Not all of these have been explicitly concerned with cognitive attributes, but all are concerned with some higher-order attributes and may be extended to the cognitive.

THEORIES OF ATTRACTION

A work of this nature is hardly the place for an exhaustive review of the ramifications and complexities of current theories of attraction. But in order to show how the present view may incorporate these theories, it is necessary to expound their main points and to re-interpret them in this light. Full justice has not therefore been done to the viewpoints (cf. Berscheid and Walster, 1969), but it is hoped that this does not imply that injustice has resulted.

Reciprocity-of-liking is one kind of explanation of attraction which seems to be concerned with 'overlap'. The suggestion of reciprocity-of-liking, stemming from popular culture and from Heider's (1958) balance theory, is that we like those who like us, or who like the same things as we do (one of which is ourselves). This raises the question of whether we like someone *because* they like us, or whether the knowledge that a person likes us merely strengthens our attraction to them, or whether we like them and then, incidentally, perceive that they like us. To have any value whatever, the theory must mean to suggest one of the first two possibilities. Curry and Emerson (1970) raise the question, in this context, of which of our 'selves' the other person should like in order to produce the effect. They argue that individuals project images and when the image projected is the one 'received', then the actor has been 'effective'. However, he is only 'successful' if his presented image is evaluated favourably. It is thus not clear whether individuals wish to be evaluated positively in terms of their projected image, their self image, or a mixture of both, or whatever. But this ambiguity serves to justify the claim that this is another example of a cue whose importance is to be regarded as subjectively evaluated, and one can therefore suggest that it becomes a filtering cue, whose significance is not 'set'. Indeed, another's liking for oneself is not automatically endearing (Berscheid and Walster, 1969) and depends not only on one believing oneself to be likeable (Jones and Schrauger, 1970), but also on the sequence in which liking and disliking may have been expressed (Aronson and Linder, 1965). Furthermore, it is not only the liking itself which can be interpreted, but also the reasons for it. Jones et al. (1968) demonstrated that ingratiators were regarded as less attractive than those who were not perceived as ingratiators.

The explanatory power of the concept of reciprocity-of-liking seems, therefore, to have its limitations. Insofar as it is intended to summarize a 'determinant' of attraction, it seems unable to do so across the board; and insofar as it describes a cue-for-evaluation which may also suggest similarity of outlook, it can be subsumed under the theory of filtering.

Matching is another kind of overlap, and derives from Level-of-Aspiration Theory (Lewin et al., 1944). The assumption of this view is that the aspiration to achieve realistic goals depends not only on the desirability of the goal but also on the perceived likelihood of its being achieved. Walster et al. (1966) suggested that romantic partners might be seen as 'goals' of some type and may therefore be subject to the same type of 'reality adjustment'. That is to say, one's selection of a romantic partner will be carried out among the pool of potentiality which contains persons who 'match' one's own estimation of a realistic goal. In many cases this will simply mean that individuals will choose as 'dates' those persons who are, for example, comparable in terms of physical attractiveness to the level at which the individual feels he belongs (Berscheid et al., 1971). However, Stroebe et al. (1971) have argued that physical attractiveness is less important as a factor in marital choice than it is as a factor in dating choice. The matching hypothesis seems therefore to apply only in a limited area of concern in the acquaintance process; or else it is a wider type of 'similarity hypothesis' and can be considered with other types below (p. 46).

Stimulus-value-role theory (Murstein, 1970, 1972) suggests that physical attractiveness plays a part in marital choice in that individuals will tend to choose partners who embody a level of attractiveness similar to their own. In this respect it is similar to the matching hypothesis. However, it goes on to claim that some kind of value-oriented perception is initiated subsequently. Thus, individuals may seek to match and to compare their cognitive evaluations on religious outlook, professional aspiration or attitudes to Vietnam, for example, as well as their actual personal values in terms of race, status or education. Marital choices are taken by this view to be determined by the extent to which homogeneity of values is apparent, and also by the degree of role compatibility which exists between prospective partners.

This position has some basic similarities to that adopted here in that it assumes a progress of stages in marital choice, but it does deal explicitly with marital choice rather than the wider context of friendship generally. It may thus have a specificity (as stated at present) which obscures the value of similar tenets elsewhere. For example, the present view would not necessarily assume that friends (as opposed to marital partners) would be *similar* in terms of physical attractiveness; but it will assert that physical cues are relevant at an early stage. Equally, it makes no assumption of homogeneity of role or status, although it does assert their relevance, but will be seen to consider the order of these stages to be role-value and not vice versa. SVR theory thus seems to be valuable as a starting point from which to elaborate and expand a similar outlook. In this case it will be incorporated in the present standpoint and extended.

In contrast, *complementarity of needs* was suggested by Winch (1958) to be the factor which determined choice of marital partners. This hypothesis states that persons who are, for example, low on dominance would tend to choose marital partners who are high on dominance, and vice versa. In other words, the claim is that individuals might seek as marital partners some person who possesses the very qualities which they themselves lack, such that each complements the other. This apparently innocuous suggestion has given rise to a furious and somewhat sterile debate on whether complementarity or similarity is the main factor; on whether the effect of complementarity is widespread, and what it applies to (needs, opinions, values, etc.); on whether similarity and complementarity are incompatible; and many other practical and conceptual problems (Rychlak, 1965; Miller et al., 1966; Wright, 1965, 1968).

However, the debate is beginning to resolve itself (Tharp, 1963; Levinger, 1964; Tharp, 1964; Wright, 1968) by a concentration on the semantic rather than the empirical issues. The distinction drawn between the two concepts is, at best, sometimes unclear, for their mutual exclusion is by no means firmly established; some confusion may have been engendered by incautious interchange of the terms 'needs', 'attitudes' and 'personality', since apparently opponent authors may have been tackling different problems. This comment may also indicate that differences may be attributable to the levels of 'friendship' discussed. Now that the conceptual issues are beginning to be clearly visualized, it is becoming the accepted view that complementarity of needs *does* obtain in some needs of some pairs of friends (and marital partners) but a basic similarity of attitudes characterizes most friendship pairs at the level investigated by most investigators (Byrne, Griffit and Stefaniak, 1967).

The similarity hypothesis is the view which has most often been contrasted with the above hypothesis and it argues (broadly) that individuals look for similarity of some type between themselves and others. But it is not similarity of any sort regardless which is sought, as has been shown by Jellison and Zeisset (1969). They found that sharing a trait (ability to taste and smell particular chemicals) with another person was viewed by subjects as attractive and inducing attraction to the other only if the trait was represented as 'desirable' and 'uncommon'.

However, the similarity hypothesis has probably generated more research than any other in this field, and the types of similarity which have been investigated are manifold (e.g. Winslow, 1937—similarity of opinions; Broderick, 1956—similarity of values; Byrne, Clore and Worchel, 1966—similarity of economic status; Miller, Campbell, Twedt and O'Connell, 1966 —similarity of reputations (same-sex pairs only); Senn, 1971—similarity of task-performance). There are, however, two main trends underlying much of the work which has been completed and these depend on similarity of attitudes and similarity of personality. Similarity—or perceived similarity —of these two measures of cognitive structure has been explained as a factor leading to friendship because it increases understanding and therefore aids communication (Runkel, 1956) and evidence to support this view has been presented by both Triandis (1959) and Menges (1969). Triandis' work showed how similarity of categorizing and structuring the relationships between particular jobs aided communication-effectiveness between supervisors and subordinates in a factory; while Menges illustrated a comparable effect when students and their teachers rated supplied statements. Byrne (1961, 1969), however, has presented the stronger view that similarity serves as 'consensual validation' for beliefs held by individuals. As may be clear from Chapter 1, this represents a formal statement of the type of hypothesis argued for there and views the individual as seeking for his close acquaintances those individuals who, because they hold a similar view of the world, thereby reinforce the attitudes (on Byrne's view) which he himself holds. An extension of this view is the one to be taken here.

With such a rationale, Byrne and coworkers have succeeded in presenting a vast amount of evidence to show that similarity of attitudes is what underlies attraction. Byrne and Nelson (1965) showed a significant positive relation between similarity of attitudes with a stranger and attraction towards him. In other words, subjects who were more similar to the stranger were likely to be more attracted to him and the authors concluded that the effect was a linear function of the number of positive reinforcements provided by the similarity of attitudes. This finding was furthered by Byrne and Rhamey (1965) who reported that attraction to a stranger was significantly increased by having him appear similar to subjects on items concerning personal attributes and evaluations. Byrne and Griffit (1969) showed that subjects were able to perceive the similarity existing between them (in some cases independently of their ability to verbalize such similarities) and they contended that although awareness of similarity could influence attraction, it was not a necessary component of the similarity-attraction relationship.

This brief summary of some of the work which has been done by Byrne and his coworkers has no more than scratched the surface of the contribution which he has made. However, it is adequate to show the success which has attended his general stance and to point up some of the main elements of the paradigm used in research on attitude-similarity.

The other line of attack on the attraction problem is one based on personality-similarity. Byrne, Griffit and Stefaniak (1967) argue that attraction is multi-determined, with several factors—they do not employ the notion of filters—playing a role (e.g. propinquity, attitude-similarity, perceived similarity etc.). In a comparison of the effects on attraction of attitude-similarity and similarity of personality-characteristics (measured on the Repression-Sensitization Scale), they found that attitude-similarity was the only one of the two which influenced attraction and therefore adopted the standpoint that attitude-similarity and not personality-similarity is of the greatest importance in mediating attraction. But, as in most of Byrne's experiments, the dependent variable is reported attraction to (sometimes hypothetical) strangers and firmly established friendships are not investigated, nor have operational measures of attraction been the general rule.

It is true, however, that research on personality-similarity has not yet been particularly convincing. Lerner, Dillehay and Sherer (1967) found that changes in perceived personality-similarity were *not* invariably causes of changes in attractiveness and this casts doubt on the strength of any relationship between the two. Hogan and Mankin (1970) present evidence that personality-similarity (measured by the California Psychological Inventory) is not as effective a determinant of general liking as it may be of 'clique liking' (see Chapter 6, p. 63). The experiments of Izard (1960 (a), (b)) using the Edwards Personal Preference Schedule have, however, succeeded in giving some support for the suggestion that mutual friends have similar personality profiles. But it is important to note that his two studies were different in outcome as a function of the type of subjects used. For when the subjects were new entrants to university and therefore when friendships had had little chance to develop, similarity on the personality test was a predictor of only unilateral sociometric choice; while it could predict mutual choices in firmly established friendships. This suggests the view, to be tested empirically later (Chapter 6), that personality-similarity, as traditionally measured, is of importance at a different stage in the development of friendship from that where similarity of other dimensions holds sway.

Nevertheless, despite the qualifications so far attached to work on personality-similarity, and the compelling and consistent nature of the work on attitudes, only confusion can follow from the view that there is any real conflict between the results and that one measure is more efficient an indicator of 'the cause' of attraction than the other. The plain inference from the discussion above is that investigators have not always made it clear that acquaintance and firm friendship may be rather different phenomena; and that the filters (as this exposition has it) which are applied at one stage are different from those applied later. Thus it is not entirely clear that the two approaches are attacking the problem at the same level and it is postulated that the incompleteness of much work on personality-similarity is due to the fact that the particular hypothesis was applied to an inappropriate situation. The case made out here is that the place for such tests as have been used so far is in the later stages of the development of friendship. One would find it intuitively difficult to imagine that people become close friends, after previously described filtering, *only* because they share similar attitudes on such wide topics as are contained in attitude scales (e.g. Vietnam, homosexual law reform, or corporal punishment). Equally, it is hard to see how, beyond the initial discovery, it could be rewarding to have such attitudes repeatedly shared and continually validated by the same person; and some suggestion of change and changing values for similarities seems necessary. It seems far more acceptable a view that this type of similarity merely lays the ground and that later disclosures of information reveal how such attitudes are woven into the web of an overall personality outlook. By including some such extension, change can be accommodated, the shifting emphases of a developing relationship can be accounted for, and a link can be provided between studies of attitude-similarity and attraction on the one hand and studies of personality-similarity and friendship on the other.

FIRST SUGGESTIONS FOR A SOLUTION

Maslow (1953), in discussing similarity of personality in marriage partners, found that couples were alike in basic but not superficial personality traits and the contention can be made that many tests that have been used to investigate similarity between friends may be of a type which is inappropriate, in a sense developed above and detailed in Chapter 6. It may be the case, therefore, that these tests have failed to show similarity of basic personality variables as a factor in the acquaintance process, simply because at this stage it is not. Equally, work on attitude-similarity has been successful at early acquaintance levels and would not be so at later ones, simply because attitude-similarity of this type is superseded as a filter cue at the later stage.

However, there is a ground for the amalgamation of these two views and experimental rationales, for one is led to extend the argument advanced so far, to include a new outlook on personality in this context. Kelly's theory of personal constructs has already been discussed (Chapter 2) as providing this new outlook. It provides the link between 'consensus' and an individual's view of the world and makes possible a synthesis of the findings on attitude-similarity and personality-similarity to some extent. For it is concerned with both the very fundamental attitudes of an individual (his fabric of meaning) and the higher level organization of such 'attitudes' into opinions on particular topics (the sort of attitudes measured by attitude scales), and also the even higher-level configurations and interconnections of all these things into the nexus of a personality. Furthermore, by basing its conceptual outlook on the personal way in which an individual interprets his environment, Kelly's PCT (Personal Construct Theory) can account even for those subjective explanations of experience which were discussed in Chapter 1 and have been regarded as 'contaminating' experiments by their odd or personal perspectives. The theory avoids the problem of continuity between the laboratory and 'real life' by assuming the same processes in both.

The adoption of this theory of personality as the standpoint from which to go forward, conjoins with the previous arguments both here and in Chapter 1, to provide the theoretical basis for attacking this 'area' afresh. In arranging the theoretical position, a holist approach has been adopted, where friendship processes are seen as firmly embedded in man's processes as a whole; and an argument based on 'man's view of the world' and a search for consensus has been elaborated. The distinction between necessary and sufficient 'causes' in the Acquaintance Process, and between the various 'stages' (see p. 38 in this process, provide for an elaborate conceptualization of the area of friendship formation (in the widest sense). One main elaboration is the putative link between processes in friendship formation and those in person perception, whose 'function' will be reconsidered. Clearly these ramifications and elaborations raise several empirical questions and these are now ready for investigation in the light of the approach which has been adopted.

5

Preliminary Investigations: The Structural Approach

Completion of the exposition of a theoretical perspective must inevitably lead on to empirical questions, many of which have already presented themselves. The perspective concentrates on comparison of constructs, on social reality and on communication: the emphasis therefore inevitably falls on *content* of constructs (i.e. the actual constructs which an individual uses) and on what is communicated. However, in taking this approach the new outlook departs somewhat from the usual trend of much PCT (Personal Construct Theory) research methodology, for in a good deal of research the Reptest is analysed on an exclusively statistical basis in the search for *structure* of individual systems (i.e. the way in which an individual interweaves the content of his constructs) rather than on content itself. One cannot simply ignore this other, predominant, approach and it therefore behoves the present enquiry at least to begin by attempting to analyse friendship by means of the statistical measures which can be derived from the Reptest. This may also be desirable as an aid to clarification of some specific problems which that kind of methodology creates in this context.

Of course, it is not suggested that any attempt at structural analysis is *a priori* unsuitable here, nor that it will prove to be of little value, but, given the emphasis of the present view, it may prove less valuable here than another method. Indeed, it was originally claimed (Chapter 2, p. 19) that part of the value of PCT lay in its simultaneous provision of two avenues for experimentation (content *and* structure), so both facets should be considered here. The former reflects the emphases of Byrne's approach on attitudes, but Tesser (1971) has shown that both the evaluative and the structural components of attitudes were positively related to attraction. So far the emphasis of much PCT research has fallen exclusively upon the measurement of structure (Bieri, 1953, 1955; Bannister, 1960, 1962, 1963; Tripodi and Bieri, 1963, 1966; Warren, 1966; Slater, 1969; Miller, 1969; Fransella, 1970; Crandall, 1970; Adams–Webber, 1970 (a), (b); Delia, Gonyea and Crockett, 1971; Epting, 1972). The sheer weight of such evidence gives a clear initial directive. Furthermore, there has been a large body of work on the statistical approach to the Reptest and several measures have been derived (Bonarius, 1965; Warren, 1966) which offer themselves as ready tools for the tackling of the problem.

Yet there is no direct evidence on the problem of interpersonal attraction which tackles the similarity hypothesis from a PCT standpoint. However, one is encouraged to look further into this topic by the tangential evidence provided by Triandis (1959). In this experiment, workers and their supervisors were asked to categorize a list of jobs. It was shown that cognitive similarity (especially 'syndetic similarity'—i.e. structural similarity in the way in which concepts were associated with other concepts) increased the effectiveness of communication. There is a clear affinity between such concepts and personal constructs.

This leads one to suspect that established friendships show greater similarities of structure than do 'nominal groups' (i.e. groups composed of individuals who are not friends with one another, but are nevertheless in the same acquainted population). For example, friends will be more similar in their arrangement of descriptions of fellow members and would thus differentiate their group from other people in a way in which a nominal group will not. This kind of differentiation is meet for analysis by statistical measures derived from the Reptest. A preliminary study with this basic hypothesis was therefore carried out (Duck, 1972).

METHOD FOR THE PILOT STUDY*

A necessary condition for the satisfactory completion of this study was the identification of a number of friends and the construction of a parallel 'nominal' group. In order to effect this selection rigorously, an initial subject-pool was created containing 40 subjects, including the 10 members of a known friendship group. All subjects were male undergraduates in the same college, in their first or second year of study at university and all were asked to indicate their personal preferences amongst the 39 other names in the original subject-pool. By such sociometric means, objective assessments of the existence of the supposed group of friends could be obtained, since these 10 subjects were the only ones who all made reciprocated choices of one another. A comparison group of 10 members was then constructed so as to include those who had expressed the fewest possible number of reciprocal choices of other members. When the friendship group and the nominal group had been satisfactorily identified by these means, all other subjects were thanked and discharged.

* A report of this experiment has previously been published in Duck, S. W., 'Friendship, Similarity and the Reptest', *Psychological Reports*, **31**, 1972, 231–234.

The two experimental groups were then given a 20×20 Reptest. This consisted of a list of 20 elements and 20 rows, in each of which a different triad was selected for construal. The element list (see Chapter 2, p. 22) contained in each case two distinct groups of 10 elements each. The first set of elements consisted of the 10 members of the subject's own group, including self. This first set of elements was thus different for the two groups of subjects. The second 10 elements were all people who, by virtue of their prominence in college, were well known to all subjects (e.g. the Bursar and members of sports teams). This second element set was included on the Reptests of both groups and was the same for them all. The particular Reptest format used here was designed to ensure that equal numbers of triads for construal were selected from each of the two element sets.

The instructions followed the usual methods (Kelly, 1955) in enjoining the subjects to construe each triad in terms of a simultaneous similarity and contrast. Examples of actual constructs generated by this means are given on page 154 and full instructions are exemplified in Appendix A. Subjects were then instructed to indicate with ticks those two elements of the triad to whom the 'similarity' part of the construct applied. However, since this study was concerned with the structure of systems, subjects were also instructed, on this occasion only, to indicate all other elements to whom the similarity pole applied. These operations (considering the triad; identifying a similarity and contrast; indicating all those to whom the similarity pole applied) constituted the essence of the test and were completed by all subjects for each of the 20 rows of the Reptest. It should once more be noted that each subject supplied his own constructs and these were not provided by the experimenter. On completion of the Reptest, subjects were thanked for their cooperation and released.

ANALYSIS OF THE REPTESTS

All completed Reptests were individually factor analysed (Kelly, 1955) until all factors had been extracted. The hypothesis is that friendship group members will differentiate the other members of their particular group from the other elements, and this can be tested as follows. First factors extracted in this analysis are viewed as the most important and central for the individual (Kelly, 1955), so members of the subject's own group should account for significantly more first factors, if our hypothesis is true. An artificial factor pattern was fabricated to reflect the kind of pattern which would have resulted from a subject's indication that the 'similarity' pole of the construct applied to the members of his group exhaustively and exclusively (cf. Method Section, above). In the friendship group this pattern predicted 55·85 per cent of the first factors but only 26·61 per cent in the nominal group. The hypothesis was supported by the finding that this difference is highly significant ($p < 0.02$). It suggests a similar cognitive structuring in the sense that subjects generated constructs which were relevant to their friends, to whomever else they also applied. It does not simply suggest that they generated similar constructs *about* one another, since this finding is independent of construct content.

Friendship is further reflected in similarity of structuring (and vice versa) in the following way, for factor analysis contains a weighting procedure by means of which the positive and negative values of a dichotomous construct are disclosed. Friends might reasonably be supposed to be associated with more positive construals than other elements; and this should mean that the members of the friendship group should attribute more positives to the first 10 elements on their Reptest than should the members of the nominal group. The relevant totals of positives were computed for each group and a White's Ranking Procedure was completed on the 20 scores. For the friendship group the sum of ranks was 65 but for the nominal group the total was 143. For $N = 20$ and one rank sum less than 71, the probability value is $P < 0.01$.

The hypothesis that similarity of structure of construct systems could differentiate a friendship group from a nominal group on Reptest measures is thus supported on two tests.

DISCUSSION AND CONCLUSIONS

The above types of analysis, stemming from some recent research approaches to PCT, have shown that when a PCT view of personality is taken, the similarity hypothesis merits closer attention. However, the form which this interest should take is not entirely clear, for it will be remembered that each subject provided his own set of constructs and these findings on structure are thus *independent of the content of the construct systems investigated*. This is important first because it points to the depths at which one can discover the similarities which may underlie a similarity hypothesis; and secondly it emphasizes the divorce between structure and content which characterizes a good deal of research in PCT.

Yet it may be claimed that the differentiation of the friendship group from other elements may reflect simple agreement on descriptions rather than similarity of construct systems. In other words, similarity of construct application may here be confused with similarity of structure. There are two counter-arguments: first, if this is so, then all well and good! For it suggests that which was argued in Chapter 1, that a social reality-base for descriptions of other humans has a high priority in any 'social animal's' requirements. The second argument is that similarity of descriptions amounts to similarity of some parts of a structural system, as the meaning of the descriptions is related to its associates and interconnections. The meaning of someone's descriptions is clarified by observation of contrasts and associations.

However, the depth of the problems raised by the similarity hypothesis can be seen from the fact that whatever constructs a given member of the friendship group may have generated, he tended to apply them to his group. It is unclear how this could be due to an artefact of the test, since the Reptests had been modified to ensure that the number of comparison triads selected from the first 10 elements was equal to the number selected from the second 10 elements. One would thus suppose that no bias had been built in to concentrate subjects on to constructs which applied especially to members of their group. Yet the analysis reveals that members of the friendship group did tend thus to apply their constructs, even in cases where the construct had been generated in consideration of three people from the second 10 elements, who were unconnected with the group. Here, then, is another example of a way in which structuring was similar, in that subjects tended to concentrate on constructs from their individual systems which applied to their friends. A similarity in the strategy of thinking is suggested.

While this supports the basic contentions of the theoretical outlook advanced in the first chapters, this suggestion has the utility of indicating the complex subtlety of the levels at which similarity can be exposed for the hypothesis. Unless subjects are gifted with Holmesian insight (Conan-Doyle, 1966), they are unlikely to have access to the types of intricacies revealed directly by such a purely statistical analysis. Their appreciation of such underlying structural similarities must in real life be mediated through content, which this analysis does not attack. While content cannot be completely dissociated from structure in a perfect analysis (since the nexus of individual content items will determine their ultimate meaning—see Chapter 2, p. 19), it may be necessary to isolate content for the moment to analyse its effects. Certainly, 'content' is that which is most closely redolent of 'attitudes' as evaluative items and as such it represents a field of study in its own right.

In some previous work on PCT the emphasis falls so heavily on structure that content often appears relegated to the status of an epiphenomenon. This may be because the work on PCT has previously had a heavy bias towards the clinical areas of psychology, whence the theory was largely derived and where Kelly felt it to be most useful. In clinical studies, analysis of the structural linkages between constructs in an individual's semantic space provides useful diagnostic information. However, it is arguable whether an emphasis on structure is quite so central to other areas. Since the concern here is one that can be seen to rest very much on the consensual validation of constructs, the emphasis very naturally begins to fall on the content side of PCT and less on the structural side.

Further justification for this shift of emphasis can be gained from the fact that early suspicion of some of the statistical measures of the Reptest analysis has not been entirely dispelled by preliminary studies at the start of this work. In brief and excursionary studies carried out as part of the experimental programme, some of the assumptions of the statistical techniques involved in Reptesting were questioned, as were some of the techniques themselves. For example, it was found that the usual injunction that, after generating constructs, subjects should put ticks or crosses for all elements on each construct as indicators of the applicability of the positive or negative pole of that construct, was an instruction which often involved subjects in difficulty. This was because they felt that the similarity pole required different contrasts when applied to different people; that is (as argued in Chapter 2) the implicitly denied characteristic is frequently made dependent on the context of application of the similarity pole. This means, in effect, that a slightly different construct is being used on each occasion and the value of ticks and crosses (with the overtones of 'standardization') is therefore lost. These shades of meaning cannot even be captured by shades of numbering. However, if the subjects are not instructed to indicate to whom the construct applies, then the problem of standardization simply disappears. Subjects merely progress through consideration of successive comparison triads and in so doing they expose further parts of their construct system, which are nonetheless parts of the system for being highly peculiar parts with only specific relevance to one or two construed elements. In addition to this problem of assumptions, physical variation in the size of the number of elements used on the Reptest was found to afflict the reliability of some measures used in the literature (e.g. Warren, 1966), and other problems attend several other of such techniques used (N. Warren, pers. comm., April, 1970). Furthermore, for statistical analysis, constructs have to be assumed to be bipolar and thus reversible, in the sense that applying the positive pole must be logically equivalent to denying the negative. This question has been discussed by Mair (1967), who found that when subjects classified items into categories based on their previously supplied positive and negative construct labels, there was some overlap of classification into categories which had previously been reported as opposites.

Such considerations as these did little to quell the doubts about 'the statistical approach' to the Reptest. Thus, although the structural side had been dealt with in no great depth here, the pilot work had had the advantage of showing that there were good reasons for looking at the content of personal construct systems more carefully. This approach has its own special problems and the first clear, if somewhat pedestrian, need is to offer some validity measures for this new approach and show how it matches other methods. For its validation is logically prior to its application to the central issue.

6

A Comparison of the Content Approach with Other Methods

INTRODUCTION

The pilot work described in the previous chapter has provided some support for the view that similarity and friendship are somehow linked and that this link is demonstrable by means of the Reptest measures. However, the statistical types of measure used there have been suggested to present not only technical but also theoretical difficulties. This type of approach will therefore be left for the moment, without prejudice to the question of its value or its possible development in this area. These questions remain for subsequent empirical investigation.

However, the above decision does not entail the abandonment of PCT (Personal Construct Theory) as an integral part of the approach, for the new outlook stressed comparison of construct content rather than system structure. Indeed, PCT itself offers a *double* line of enquiry (structure *and* content) and the basis for relinquishing structural analysis was only this: that it is surface content rather than underlying structure which is available, in the normal course of events, to individuals in everyday life. So, although it will become possible later to offer theoretical suggestions which redintegrate the two (Chapter 11), the emphasis of the studies now falls on content similarity.

A methodology which analyses construct content is somewhat of a new one and is not without its practical problems, as will appear. Inevitably the first task is to tackle the pedestrian but necessary questions which arise early in connection with any such departure from the usual emphases. The most basic of these questions is, of course, whether the approach actually works! This is not long in the proof. Also important is the problem of how the approach fares *vis à vis* other established approaches. In the present case, the question is a two-edged one: how does the content approach fare *vis à vis* the structural approach which has just been shown to have value? and how does it fare with respect to independent tests, such as those on attitudes and personality? Fortunately, these lugubrious questions have, in this instance, certain added theoretical interest: they can be asked because of their face value but also can assist the development of the hypothesis. The reason is not hidden under a bushel. It has been claimed that evaluative and attitude similarity may be an important influence on the course of early acquaintanceships, but that the emphasis in these relationships will edge slowly towards examination of amounts of personality similarity and, ultimately, towards consideration of the extent of construct similarity. For this reason, the hypothesis predicts that later, established relationships will be characterized by similarity of personal constructs which will be less apparent in the case of nominal pairs. Conversely, it was claimed earlier that attitude tests may be inappropriate for use on firmly established friendships: in short, attitude-value similarity was claimed to have no powers of differentiating between established friendship pairs and nominal pairs, if measured when friendships have become established and nominal pairs have implicitly rejected the possibility of friendships with their 'nominal partners'. For this reason, a comparison of the powers of an attitude-value test and of the Reptest is clearly a valuable one. If the Reptest differentiates where the attitude test cannot, then at one stroke the value of the Reptest is enhanced; the utility of a content approach *vis à vis* the structural approach is implicitly supported; and a major assumptive component of the model is given some early support. If, on the other hand, the attitude scale has powers equal to or superior to those of the Reptest, then this will of necessity become an embarrassingly shortened book!

At this stage a basic 'correlational' method would seem to serve the purposes before us rather more adequately than any other and the same kind of design may be used as in the pilot study. This will involve as subjects a set of individuals who have already formed friendships whose existence has become firmly established. In mirroring the design of the pilot study, comparison between the two kinds of measure (structure and content) is facilitated, in that the question in both cases is the same: Can the measures derived from PCT distinguish friendship pairs from randomly constituted 'nominal pairs'? Thus the present problem is merely to establish a measurable relationship between similarity and friendship and the question of the direction of causality in this relationship is reserved for later empirical consideration (Chapter 7).

Accordingly, Experiment A was a comparison of the powers of the Reptest and an attitude-values test: the Allport–Vernon Study of Values.

METHOD FOR EXPERIMENT A: CONSTRUCTS AND ATTITUDES

It was a clear aim of this experiment that subjects should be well acquainted with one another and, to this end, subjects were recruited amongst the senior psychology class at Glasgow. This ensured that all 26 subjects had known each other for three or four years and had encountered one another in a variety of academic and social situations. In order more formally to establish the friendship patterns in the group, sociometric techniques were employed as part of the experiment. Of the 26 subjects, 14 were male and 12 female and all subjects were in the age range 21–24 except for one member of the class who was a mature student.

Subjects completed the Allport–Vernon Study of Values which requires a measure of agreement to be expressed about certain attitude and evaluative statements. No instructions were given to supplement those provided on the standard test booklet (Richardson, 1965). Subjects also completed a Reptest. The method of the study required a form of the Reptest (Kelly, 1955) where only the content of constructs was to be considered and subjects were therefore not asked to provide any data for structural analysis: that is, they were asked only to generate constructs and not to place ticks under the names of those to whom the constructs applied. (The reader is referred to Appendix A for the details of the elements and instructions used here.) When a 16 × 18 form of the test had been completed, sociometric techniques were used to elicit a list of 'friends in this class'. When this test had been completed, subjects were thanked for participating and were dismissed.

ANALYSIS AND RESULTS

The sequence of analyses adopted in this experiment was that which was observed in most of the experiments reported here and many of the caveats given here will apply equally later on, even if not explicitly evoked. The first part of the analysis was of the sociometric data. All choices on this test were scrutinized and attention was subsequently concentrated on those choices which had been reciprocated (A chose B; B chose A). The reason is that in a study of this sort it is plainly perverse to class unreciprocated choices as representative of established friendship. In this instance, the decision resulted in the exclusion of one female subject who had made no choices which were reciprocated.

It is clear that this analysis must undermine the criticism that friendship choices were artefactually induced or randomly generated, since the mean length of the list of friends was low ($\bar{X} = 4.9$, including unreciprocated choices). If the choices were randomly expressed, then one would presumably find longer lists, with many excess unreciprocated (random) choices. It will appear later that this is lower than the usual mean for such lists, and this may, to an extent, be due to the fact that choices were restricted within the class. This constraint was later abandoned and subjects were allowed to choose from the general range of acquaintances, when the mean was usually found to be around 6·5 *reciprocated* choices. Incidentally, it is useful here to show why it does not matter that the subjects were students of psychology, since the dangers are well known. It will become clear that the subsequent analysis concerns similarity *between* tests and since they were completed independently, this is the kind of relationship which cannot have been manipulated—even by these trainee psychologists!

The analysis then proceeded to deal with the data from the Study of Values. To complete this analysis each test was marked individually (Richardson, 1965) and the score on each of 6 attitude dimensions was derived for each subject. When all subjects' data had been computed, consideration was given to the discovery of whether a given dimension offered a basis for differentiating friendship and nominal pairs. For this stage of the analysis, each subject's data in turn took on the role of 'comparison data' and his score on the dimension concerned was subtracted from every other subject's corresponding score in turn. Thus, the smaller the difference between two scores, the greater the similarity of the two subjects on that attitude dimension. Each of these resulting difference scores was classified in turn into one of two categories, according to whether this pair of subjects had chosen each other on the sociometric test or not. Thus, for each subject, two categories of scores for each dimension were derived, one from the friendship pairs of which he was a member and one from the nominal pairs. A mean for each of these categories was then computed for each subject. When all subjects' data had been treated in this way for a given dimension, and all subjects' means had been derived as above, a paired *t*-test was performed on the 25 sets of two means. This provided a general measure of whether the difference between two subjects' scores was related to whether they had chosen each other on the sociometric test or not. If similarity on the dimension concerned were a basis for friendship, then a significant result should be found, indicating smaller differences (and therefore greater similarity) between the scores of pairs of friends than between the scores from the nominal pairings. All 6 dimensions were individually treated in this manner, yet in no case did the results achieve a level of significance. That is to say, in no case did any of the attitude dimensions succeed in differentiating friendship pairs from nominal pairs in terms of similarity.

This is initial encouragement for the viewpoint here, but the crucial test yet remains. It is now of central importance whether the Reptest is able to differentiate friendship pairs from nominal pairs by showing that friends have more similar constructs. In order to test the value of the Reptest on this point, the following analysis was completed. Since this was the basic method of analysis of all the experiments reported later (except where indicated) it is reported at length here and summarized in Appendix B.

Each Reptest was first taken individually and prepared for analysis. This entailed the erasure of every construct on that grid which exactly and literally repeated any other on the grid. For example, if a subject used the construct 'Tall–Short' four times, three instances would be erased. This meant that only one instance of each construct was allowed to remain and this was because the content of the constructs rather than their frequency was of interest at this point. When this preparation had been made for all Reptests in the sample, it was possible to enumerate the similarities between pairs of Reptests. At this stage in the development of the experimental programme, only one widely based criterion for similarity between constructs was used, namely: 'conceptual similarity', although later (see Chapter 7) it proved useful to distinguish between this and another. The concept criterion involved classifying as similar any two constructs which expressed the same idea in the same or different words. Thus, for examples, 'Male–Female' on one Reptest was counted similar to 'Male–Female' on another; 'Always laughing–Always sad' was counted as similar to 'Cheerful person–Always sad'; 'Say what they feel–Tends to hide emotions' was counted similar to 'Express feelings readily—Reserved in expression of feelings'. (At this stage in the series of experiments, constructs were counted for practical purposes as similar whether in the same sequence or reversed—e.g. 'Male–Female' was counted as similar to 'Male–Female' *or* to 'Female–Male'. The validity of this assumption rests on the fact that the implicit evaluative or affective aspects of construct polarities were not of such concern here as were the dimensions themselves. However, there are certain other theoretical issues associated with this assumption, common to this and other studies, both with the Reptest—e.g. Mair, 1967—and with other personality measures—e.g. Hoffman and Maier, 1966. These implications will be discussed in Chapter 11.) Three independent raters achieved a reliability as measured by Kendall's coefficient of concordance (w) on rating for construct similarity here of $w = 0.7594$ ($p < 0.01$).

Each pair of constructs was rated into one of the categories 'similar' or 'not similar' to one another and the number of similarities between all possible pairings of subjects was recorded. The similarity scores were classified, as the attitude scores had been earlier, into those originating from friendship pairings and those from nominal pairings, and mean scores for each category were derived for each of the 25 subjects. A student's t-test was carried out on these 25 pairs of means and gave $t = 4.7259$, $df = 24$, $p < 0.001$, which gives powerful evidence that the Reptest is able to differentiate friendship and nominal pairs.

This confirms the second aim of the study and supports the view that the PCT approach is able to uphold the similarity hypothesis when content of construct systems is considered, just as it can when a 'structural' attack is made (Chapter 5). The two lines of approach to the similarity-hypothesis which were derived from PCT thus compare favourably with one another, and although the 'structural' method is a well-tried and tested derivative of PCT (see Chapter 5), the new content method is worth further investigation, and will be adopted as the main method here.

However, a further aim of the study was to offer a direct comparison of the Reptest and the Study of Values, and in order to effect the relative evaluation of the two approaches the results of this analysis were submitted to a Mann Whitney U test, with conversion to Z scores (Hays, 1963). This gave $Z = 2.59$, $P < 0.005$. This compounds the earlier 'eyeball' evidence that the Reptest is superior to the attitude test when it comes to differentiating established friendship pairs from nominal pairs in terms of similarity.

DISCUSSION OF EXPERIMENT A AND INTRODUCTION TO EXPERIMENT B

The discovery that pairs of friends may be differentiated from nominal pairs by analysis of the similarities of the content of their construct systems is in itself of major importance for the present outlook. For it both indicates that the newly adopted content methods compare favourably with the usual structural kinds of analysis of the Reptest and also suggests that the arguments advanced earlier are at least justifiable hypotheses for more intensive study. The evidence is that the methodology and the rationale have the utility which is required of them and justify further ramification. The results indicate that PCT methods can be applied fruitfully to the area of interpersonal attraction. Indeed, it has been pointed out in the previous chapters that success in this field is a rare occurrence for personality theories and these initial signs are most encouraging. It suggests that PCT's utility here would be further illuminated in an examination of its abilities *vis à vis* other personality tests and the next experiment will take this point as its focus.

However, the main value of the present results lies in their first support for the filtering hypothesis which derives from the basic position. For there is the suggestion here that the discriminant abilities of the 'cognitive' tests used in this area will be largely determined by their appropriateness to the temporal developments of the relationship under study. Naturally, such an interesting possibility as this will form a major theme in the subsequent empirical tests in this series.

For further preliminary test of the detail of the filtering hypothesis one needs to recall the arguments of Chapter 4. It was suggested there that relationships may be characterized by progression from global to more molecular cognitive assessments. In other words, that there is a shift from concern over general and undifferentiating characteristics to those which are increasingly peculiar to a particular individual. In functional terms this means there will be a shift from the concentration on attitudes towards more of an interest in personality characteristics, in established relationships. This possibility finds some support in these results.

Such a position may, however, be further refined. For it can be maintained that, when the stage of concern over personality characteristics has been reached, there may be further differentiation within this general concern. In other words, concern about general personality characteristics may precede and then cede to concern over specificities and minute detail. While filtering purposes may initially be served by summarizing the overall pattern of another's personality and assessing it for similarity, this process may yield to scrutiny of the fine weft of the fabric. If it is initially valuable and predictively valid to assess a person in terms of, say, Neuroticism or Dominance or Tolerance, etc., and to establish the degree of similarity to one's own position on such measures, it may nevertheless become more important subsequently to examine the basic material on which such assessments were founded. In our present idiom, this basic material may be seen in terms of personal constructs. Such a view would yield the prediction that, in established friendships, tests which assess personality in global terms on such dimensions as those exemplified above, may be less powerful than that which taps personal constructs. In other words, a further and more exact kind of 'appropriateness' of test to phenomena is suggested. When it comes to assessing the influence of personality similarity on friendship choice, some personality tests will prove to be more powerful at some stages in the development of the relationship than they will be at others. If such a result were found to be the case, then a good deal of help could be given on the question of why examinations of personality similarity in this field have been so equivocal. Perhaps sometimes the failure of a test to show the effects may have been due to its use in inappropriate circumstances.

In order to test this proposition, we need to compare two personality tests on a population where friendships have become indisputably established.* Equally clear is the need, for this suggestion, to compare the Reptest with a personality test which offers global descriptions of personality in terms of positions on dimensions. This much would establish many of the required points of the hypothesis. However, speculation could be given more power if the comparison demonstrated the superiority of the Reptest over a test which is one of those rare ones which has had some success in this field.

It may seem that this poses a difficult problem, but in fact there is a study which has not only used a test of the desired type in the required circumstances, but also allowed constructed groups to interact over a period (Hogan and Mankin, 1970). Subjects who had completed a CPI (California Psychological Inventory) were randomly assigned to groups ('cliques') for discussion,

---

* A more powerful test of this hypothesis, comparing the powers of Reptest and CPI on Acquainted and Unacquainted populations is available in: Duck, S.W., 'Personality similarity and friendship choice: similarity of what, when?' *Journal of Personality*, in press.

after which they were asked to rate other subjects for liking. Similarity of personality was suggested to correlate with 'clique liking', but 'general liking' was found to be related to factors in interaction styles. These results therefore confirm the *possibility* of progressively different emphases within an overall process at different levels of acquaintance, but provide no evidence about the emphases involved during the establishment of firm friendships. This result therefore encourages the investigation of the types of point raised earlier, by means of comparing the traditionally based CPI and the Reptest for 'appropriateness'. The antithesis between the rationales of the CPI (which is a means of deriving global dimensional descriptions of personality) and that of the Reptest (which relies on the individual's own semantic and cognitive categories) provides just the sort of basis which was earlier required for their empirical antithesis in this case. The confrontation will provide a further trial of the 'appropriateness' of various measures at different points in the process of attraction. For this type of appropriateness is the sort which entails measuring at the different points in a developing friendship, those aspects of it and of the other person which are subjectively relevant. Thus, the prediction is that, despite its heuristic success with constructed groups (in Hogan and Mankin, described above), the CPI will *not* differentiate friendship pairs from 'nominal' pairs in a study of established groups. Earlier claims can be supported by a demonstration that these same subjects can nevertheless be thus differentiated by a more powerful measure of those elements of personality which are more subjectively important at that point of friendship.

METHOD FOR EXPERIMENT B*

It was a clear aim of this experiment that subjects should be previously acquainted with one another, and to this end subjects were enlisted in a large student hall of residence. This in itself does not guarantee that the aim of the test would be fulfilled and so some preliminary screening was performed in order to ensure that the subject-pool contained several reasonably large groups of friends. In order to verify these affinities within the pool of subjects, a sociometric test was administered as part of the experiment. All 40 subjects (29 female and 11 male) were trainee teachers aged between 18 and 23 years, who had lived in the hall for at least one year. (This, incidentally, goes some of the way to explaining a marked 'alphabetical' influence which was manifest in this data (given as Table 3.1, p. 33). For in the first year of residence, members of the hall were assigned

* Another form of this report has appeared in: Duck, S. W., 'Similarity and perceived similarity of personal constructs as influences on friendship choice', *British Journal of Social and Clinical Psychology*, **1973** (12) pp. 1–6.

to blocks on the basis of alphabetical position of their surname. However, this does not explain their *choices* (Warr, 1965), it merely suggests an additional sociological influence on their range of acquaintances. The central question remains that of accounting for the particular choices *within* the range of acquaintances.)

Subjects first completed the CPI and were instructed to follow the printed instructions issued with the standard question booklet which comprises the test (Gough, 1964). No additional instructions were given at this stage, but during the course of the test it became apparent that some subjects were experiencing difficulty over the meaning of some American usages, such as 'hookey' and 'deportment marks'. Explanations were offered for items of this sort, and subjects then completed the test.

Next, subjects were given a 16 × 18 form of the Reptest and were given the list of elements and the instructions which are both contained in Appendix A. On completion of this test, sociometric techniques were used to elicit a list of 'friends in Sheffield' (the city where this study was conducted). Subjects were not instructed to restrict their choices to members of their hall of residence, nor was it indicated that these were the names of most interest for the subsequent analysis. A further test, relevant in Experiment C, was then completed and subjects were then thanked and paid for taking part.

ANALYSIS AND RESULTS

The first part of the analysis was of the sociometric data. All choices made on this test were scrutinized and any choices which were directed towards persons outside the range of the subject-pool were ignored. Moreover, attention was again concentrated on those choices within the pool which had been reciprocated. Concentration on established friendships and reciprocated choices resulted in the exclusion of two female subjects who had recorded no reciprocated choices and the analysis henceforth deals with the remaining 38 subjects. A sociometric choice matrix was then constructed for reference during the analysis.

Inspection of this data (given as Table 3.1, p. 33) made it quite clear that this analysis vitiates two possible criticisms of the method described above. For it may be felt that artificial 'groups' could be arrived at if a single person was made the centre of choices by other subjects. While all the 'peripheral' subjects may choose the central person (it may be held), it is possible that these 'peripheral' subjects may not choose one another and an apparent group would, in reality, disappear if the central popular person were removed. However, there are three arguments against this position: first, that groupings were not of concern so much as pairings (as will become clearer in the subsequent analysis); second, that the above decision to discount unreciprocated choices has already rendered this situation unlikely; and third, that in any case (as appears from Table 3.1), several internally cohesive groups of fairly consistent size are revealed by the analysis. This is also the vindication of the selection procedures and the evidence on which the claim to study established friendships should be seen to rest.

The second possible criticism which the data in Table 3.1 serve to undermine is that having all subjects in a single room during the sociometric test may have increased the chances of the subjects choosing from within the pool. To counter this is the view that, if this were the case, a greater random scattering (and therefore more unreciprocated choices) would have been expected. But as can be seen from the table, there is every appearance of coherence in the independent groupings of friends observed. Furthermore, the interest in reciprocated choices renders this less plausible, since, in the light of the selection procedures and the exclusion of unreciprocated choices from the definition of friendship, it is difficult to see what this criticism amounts to. Also, in view of comments made by subjects during post-experimental debriefing and the methods used in subject selection, it is strongly suggested that such criticisms cannot be upheld.

The analysis then proceeded to the derivation of scores on the 18 dimensions of the CPI for the subsequent analysis (such as 'Sociability', 'Femininity', 'Tolerance', etc.). For this, the subject's answer sheet was treated in a manner similar to that employed in the analysis of the attitude test in Experiment A. Initially, each subject's raw data were used in conjunction with a special scoring template for each of the personality dimensions and the total number of correspondences between template and answer sheet was recorded (Gough, 1964). This correspondence total represents the subject's score on the dimension and it can then be standardized. When all subjects' scores on a given dimension had been computed, an analysis was performed to discover whether a dimension, thus derived, offered a basis for differentiating friendship and nominal pairs (i.e. are friends more similar on any given dimension than are non-friends?). The method used here was essentially similar to that employed in the previous experiment (see p. 60). That is to say, the difference between a subject's score and each other subject's score was derived and then classified into the 'friendship' or 'nominal' category, and the subject's scores in these categories were reduced to means. When all subjects' data had been treated in this way for a given dimension and all subjects' means had been derived, a paired t-test was performed on the 38 sets of two means. This provided a general measure of whether the difference between two subjects' scores was related to whether they had chosen each other on the sociometric test or not. If so, one would predict that the differences between friends' score would be smaller; that is, similarity would be greater. All 18 dimensions were individually treated in this manner, yet of the 18 tests only one (using the dimension of Self-Acceptance) reached a level of significance ($p < 0.05$).

As a final test on the power of the CPI in this area (when consideration is given to established friendships), a unitary 'summary' of personality-similarity was derived. In order to compute this total, one score for the friendship category and one for the nominal category was computed for each subject in turn. This was effected by averaging the scores previously assigned to each category on each dimension; the legitimacy of which procedure rests on the fact that, at this stage, mean differences between scores on different dimensions and not the raw scores themselves were being averaged. The 38 pairs of means which this procedure generated were then subjected to a paired t-test, which gave a value of $t = 0.4855$ ($df = 37$, NS).

When firmly established friendships are examined, the results of Hogan and Mankin (1970) are not replicated in that the CPI does not offer a basis for differentiating friendship pairs from nominal pairs, either when tested by means of its 18 constituent dimensions or when reduced to a unitary measure. Only the dimension of Self-Acceptance provided any basis for differentiation. One hypothesis of the study is thus confirmed.

Much of the future of filtering theory at this stage hinges on the fate of the second prediction of this experiment: that the Reptest will again prove to be a more appropriate rationale with which to test the stage at which friendships have formed; and it will reveal a greater power of differentiating friendship pairs from nominal pairs. In order to test the value of the Reptest on this point, the standard analysis was completed, as it was in the last experiment (see p. 61). In this case, the results of the t-test on the 38 pairs of means gave $t = 2.279$, $df = 37$, $p < 0.05$, which again evidences the ability of the Reptest to differentiate friendship and nominal pairs.

A direct comparison between the powers of the two tests was effected by means of the Wilcoxon Test for the Unpaired Case, which gave $W = 37$, $p < 0.01$ and supports the view that the Reptest is superior to the CPI in these circumstances.

DISCUSSION OF EXPERIMENT B AND INTRODUCTION TO EXPERIMENT C

The confirmation of both major hypotheses derived from the original position provides useful evidence for the 'filtering' hypothesis described earlier. The suggestions of Hogan and Mankin (1970) were not supported when firm friendships were studied and of the 19 measures derived from the CPI (i.e. 18 dimensions plus one 'unitary' derivation) only the dimension of Self-Acceptance yielded a significant result. There is a well-established relationship between acceptance of self and acceptance of others (Marlowe and Gergen, 1970) and this result indicates no differently. Indeed it suggests that level of self-acceptance may be a powerful filter of populations of potential friends and since it is a dimension which appears to offer a description of a person at a very general level and one where *changes* are likely to be on a small scale, from time to time, there seems every reason for assuming that its effects may not be reduced by continued interaction. However, this is the only dimension of the test which yielded a significant result.

The results on the other specific issues tackled here justify the continued investigation of the method of studying construct content and further support the claims that personality-similarity can be shown to be related to friendship formation when a PCT outlook is taken. Indeed, there is ample evidence that the results found here are accountable in large measure to the differences in rationales and emphasis embodied in the two tests. The advantages of the Reptest over the CPI at this stage, seem to depend on its emphasis on the more personally relevant items of cognitive furniture.

It is worthy of note that the similarity measured with each test was of a different type (a point whose implications are taken up later—Chapter 11). For in one case the content similarity between generated constructs was recorded (the words used), and in the other case similarity of marks on a test (the numbers scored). Thus in the second case, it may have been possible for subjects with different answers to sets of particular questions to achieve a similar score without any great agreement existing between them on the particular items. However, in pointing this out it is pertinent to record that not only has this method of measuring personality and personality similarity been used frequently by several investigators (Izard, 1960; Hoffman and Maier, 1966; Byrne, Ervin and Lamberth, 1970) but also that any dimensional test of personality relies upon the same measuring technique for summarizing personality. The same criticism as applies to this derivation of similarity also applies to the derivation of personality which is possible from such a test: namely, that it may obscure many points of interest which PCT derivatives here tackle at a precise level. Thus, so far from being an acceptable criticism of this study, it makes the point again that a PCT rationale is a more powerful tool; and thus it provides further intuitive support for the empirical evidence already presented.

This evidence has already shown justification of the *ex hypothesi* assumption that subjects had reached a point of concern over personality-similarity. But it is clearly a concern of a refined sort since one personality test was successful and one was less of a success. This finding is a challenging one, in view of its possible relevance to the equivocation which has surrounded the study of the influence of personality similarity on friendship and interpersonal attraction. However, it is a little early, despite this encouraging sign, to draw too many conclusions. Further studies in this series cast light before this issue and it will be revived in later chapters.

It is important at this point to reassert the relevance of the consensual validation argument (Chapters 1 and 4) to what has been shown. For, at the moment, a serious criticism of the findings, and one that poses an empirical question, is whether subjects perceive the similarity which exists between them and their known friends. It was argued earlier that one reason for abandoning the 'structural' approach was that subjects could not reasonably be expected to have access to the information that their construct systems were statistically and structurally similar. But if they cannot perceive *content* similarity which exists between them, or if they make significant errors and underestimate what exists, then the basis of this approach collapses and the consensual validation argument is untenable with respect to constructs; since if they are unaware of similarities, they are probably not regarding them as important and therefore probably not using them as a basis for their validation of their 'view of the world'. Accordingly, a test was designed to examine subjects' ability to perceive any similarity of content that may exist in firmly established friendships.

METHOD FOR EXPERIMENT C

Experiment C was conducted contemporaneously with Experiment B and the same subjects were used. After they had completed the sociometric test and the subsequent 16×18 Reptest described above (pp. 64–65), subjects were given a further test which has not yet been fully described. This was intended as a test of subjects' accuracy and ability to perceive similarity between their own construct system and those of their friends. To satisfy this aim, each subject was provided with a sheet of paper whose lines had been numbered to coincide with single rows on the recent Reptest one for one. It was stressed that this correspondence was to be preserved throughout the next part of the experiment. The subjects were instructed to consider each of their elicited constructs in turn and to mark down the names of any of their acquaintances (not just 'friends') who, in their opinion, would use the same construct ('way of categorizing people') in any context—that is, not just to apply to the specific people who had actually been considered on that row where the construct was elicited. In other words, the subjects' familiarity with their acquaintances' construct systems was being tapped, and not their impressions of how far particular opinions of particular individuals were shared. To leave out a name was to suggest that the person did not use the construct and, for this reason, subjects were permitted to write 'Everyone' where they felt a construct was universal and 'No-one' where it was peculiar to themselves. When this was completed subjects were thanked and paid for taking part, as previously mentioned.

ANALYSIS AND RESULTS

In view of the relationship between this experiment and Experiment B, the data for the analysis had already been largely prepared. During this analysis, therefore, use was made of the previously derived sociometric choice matrix and of the practice of using the prepared Reptests (i.e. those where superfluous instances of constructs had been removed, for the reasons given above, p, 61) rather than the 'raw' ones.

Data from the last part of the experiment were treated as follows. For each friend chosen by a given subject it was possible to decide whether he had or had not used any of the constructs which the subject himself had used. Thus for each construct used on a given Reptest, reference could be made to the results of the test on perception of similarity and the whole range of a subject's chosen friends could be inspected for that construct and assigned to one of four exhaustive and mutually exclusive categories. These categories were:

(1) Subject named as a user of a construct some chosen friends who did in fact use it;
(2) Subject alleged the use of a construct which the person indicated did not use;
(3) Subject did not name someone as a user of a particular construct and the person did not use it;
(4) Subject omitted the name of someone who did share a common construct with him.

Scores, thus categorized, could be arranged into a 2×2 table for each subject and submitted to a Fisher's Exact Probability Test. Each subject's table was examined separately and the largest value of p in any table was $p < 0.02$. This indicates non-randomness in each table and from examination of Table 6.1 it can be seen that subjects were about twice as likely to be accurate than inaccurate (categories 1 and 3 above), but that errors were predominantly made in category 2 above. This latter result shows that, where errors are made, a tendency to perceive co-extension of construct systems is apparent, even though this co-extension does not exist.

Table 6.1. Percentages of accurate and erroneous perceptions of similarity as a function of the true position (pooled data)

| | | True position | |
		Similar	Not similar
Perceptions	Accurate	64·76	64·64
	Erroneous	35·24	35·36
		100·00	100·00

Breakdown of erroneous perceptions
Claiming similarity where none exists: 93·57 % of all errors
Denying similarity where similarity exists: 6·43 % of all errors

DISCUSSION

This study, as a part of Experiment B, has already demonstrated that actual similarities are observable between friends' construct systems when content is measured, as discussed earlier. It has also here shown that subjects are quite accurate in perceiving whether similarity exists or not, but that errors tend to be made in the direction of overestimating similarity.

The charge that the relevant task was one which subjects could not understand can be countered by observing that this would be expected to lead to *random* errors, while the results of the individual tests here showed convincingly that errors were *not* random. Equally, it is clear that subjects were not 'set' by the instructions to find similarities, since the lengths of lists varied not only between subjects but also within single lists, as a function of the specific construct considered. This indicates that subjects were able to satisfy the instructions and were not merely giving random responses in a situation which they could not grasp.

The results can therefore be seen to offer support for the consensual validation argument. For when not being accurate, subjects tended to overestimate the similarity which existed between them and their friends and this implies that the similarity is surrounded with a subjective importance, irrespective of any incidental interest which it may have.

The finding thus offers another link between PCT and the work of Byrne, mentioned earlier. Byrne and Griffit (1969) found that perceived similarity of answers on a Repression–Sensitization scale had the effect of increasing the amount of liking felt for a stranger, as a function of amounts of similarity perceived. However, it is once more salutary to note two important differences between that study and the one reported here (apart from the different empirical methods used: correlational and experimental—see Chapters 3 and 4). In the present study firmly established friendships were being explored, while Byrne and Griffit made attraction to strangers the focus of their concern. Secondly, Byrne and Griffit measured attraction as the dependent variable (i.e. they measured attraction as a function of perceived similarity), while the present study measured perceived similarity as a function of friendship.

It is important to notice the differences which this points out, for attraction to strangers has here been argued not to be mediated by precisely the same processes as those which may provide the firmer basis on which friendships can flourish and continue. This raises the 'mainstream' empirical topic of studying *developing* friendships which will shortly become the main focus of concern in this series of studies. The studies so far reported have shown fairly consistent and unitary evidence, but, on re-analysis of some of the data of the present study it was discovered that some differences in 'friendship styles' could be discerned between the sexes. For it was found that the female subjects were contributing to the effect of actual personality-similarity more than were the males. Accordingly, the data from the two sexes were taken separately and analysed as above (p. 61), such that similarities between friendship pairs and nominal pairs were considered in respect of same-sex friendship and nominal pairs and likewise in respect of different-sex pairs (Table 6.2). In both same-sex and different-sex pairs of which they were members, female subjects showed highly significant differences between scores from friendship and nominal pairs ($p < 0.002$). On the other hand, male subjects manifested this difference only in respect of same-sex friendship and nominal pairs ($p < 0.05$).

Table 6.2. Comparison of 'friendship' and 'nominal' mean similarity scores as a function of sex of chooser and sex of chosen (Sex of chooser, M or F, is given first)

	Friendship mean similarity score	Nominal mean similarity score	t
M–M	0·6762	0·4745	2·4342*
M–F	0·8182	0·7629	0·788 n.s.
F–F	1·0669	0·8883	5·684**
F–M	0·7717	0·1877	4·5432**

* $P < 0.05$; $df = 10$. ** $P < 0.002$; $df = 26$.

Duck, S. W. (1973). 'Similarity and perceived similarity of personal constructs as influences on friendship choice', *British Journal of Social and Clinical Psychology*, 12, 1–6.
Reproduced by permission of the British Psychological Society.

Table 6.3. Comparison of friendship mean similarity scores for same-sex
and different-sex friendship pairs

| | Sex of chosen | | |
Sex of chooser	Male	Female	t-value
Male	0·6762	0·8182	0·3932 NS
Female	0·7717	1·0669	2·7330 *

* $p < 0·02$, $df = 26$.

However, when different-sex choices were compared with same-sex choices across the board for each subject (Table 6.3), female subjects showed significantly greater similarity with same-sex friends ($p < 0·02$). So while females are similar in construing to friends of either sex, the amounts of similarity are greater for friends who are also female. There were no significant differences for male subjects.

This analysis shows that similarity of construct systems distinguishes same-sex friendship pairs from same-sex nominal pairs and is entirely consistent with previous findings. But with respect to different-sex friends, only female subjects appear to use construct similarity as a factor in their choices (see Table 6.3). This suggests that although both sexes use the same apparent cognitive strategy for choosing friends of the same sex, when it comes to choosing friends of the opposite sex, males and females use different 'filter' strategies. Females appear to look for similarity of construct systems in both cases, yet males do so only when choosing male friends and look for something else when choosing between potential female friends. The age and accompanying orientation of the subjects in this study may go some of the way both towards a partial explanation and towards the generation of several questions for later discussion (Chapter 11 and 12). However, there are differences not only in kind (in the case of males) but also of degree (in the case of females) in these strategies.

This finding has many labyrinthine implications, which can be discussed more fully in Chapter 12, when more evidence from the later studies has been brought to bear. It is especially interesting in that consistent sex differences have previously eluded investigators in this field (Little, 1969), where study has been directed to construct 'types' (see Chapter 7) rather than to the sorts of strategy discussed here. The present finding suggests the merit of studies of the development of construct similarity in engaged or married couples (for the implication here is that the female partner may look for similarity, even if the male partner does not. This is some evidence other than folklore for the phenomenon of 'female intuition'!). The way in which this discrepancy in strategies may be resolved is also of interest. Other developmental and demographic possibilities will be reviewed later, but for the present the study has pointed in a specific direction for further enquiry.

CONCLUSIONS

This series of experiments has shown the validity of a content-based derivative of PCT as a tool in the field of friendship formation. It has thus offered support for the basic position argued in the earlier chapters. However, besides this essential evidence, the series has also indicated the empirical importance of the distinction made in Chapter 4 between functionally and logically distinct points in the process of acquaintance. In its recent disclosure of the possible differences in friendship strategies at a supremely subtle level, the latest study offers some exciting possibilities for bringing research back into real life, since the implications for marriage guidance remain to be examined. Indeed the implications suggested by these studies are too numerous and too finely arborized to be followed up properly in one single short programme of research. Regrettably, therefore, it is necessary to confine the progress of the argument to particular aspects of the hypothesis. In this respect, a prime candidate for choice would be a depth study of the generic changes in focus which occur within the various kinds of developed friendship in terms of norms or construct similarity. Another line would clearly be a study of the changes which occur from beginning to formation in friendship. This choice will be taken, since no evidence has yet been presented to discover whether similarity precedes or follows friendship and this is clearly important to the development of the current position. In taking this course, due deference will be paid to these latest results on different strategies in the sexes, and so it may prove to be more fruitful to reduce the area of possible friendship choice to contain only those of a subject's own sex. This choice directs us towards a longitudinal study of the development of friendship patterns in single-sex groups.

7

A Longitudinal Study of Developing Friendship Patterns

INTRODUCTION

It would indeed be unfortunate if the inevitably prosaic nature of the last chapter's validity testing were to obscure the possible value of some of its results. For the studies so far reported have not been without importance for the development of the argument and many aspects of them will later be seen in another guise. They have so far succeeded in accrediting the method which has been adopted and have satisfied the requirement that the basic theoretical proposals should have empirical validity. However, the last study in particular has also had more to offer. It has indicated differences between the underlying strategies of friendship choice in the two sexes, when the choices are expressed within a mixed-sex population. Further, it has suggested the usefulness of a longitudinal study of friendship patterns as they develop. This latter method will help to clarify whether similarity of constructs is largely a product or a cause of friendship choice. But it would have additional incidental effects beside the main outcome outlined above, not least of which would be the provision of a set of results which would be complementary to the validity tests. They could give some indication of the reliability of Reptest techniques, during any possible changes which may occur as a function of the development of friendship from mere acquaintance to an established relationship. Such a study will thus seek to provide evidence on the suggestion made earlier (Chapter 6, p. 63) that PCT (Personal Construct Theory) may be a method which is of use at the earlier stages of acquaintance as well as at later stages.

In view of the clear suggestions of Experiment C that choice strategies differ in the two sexes when cross-sex pairings are considered, it was decided to tackle the problem of a longitudinal study by investigating a male subject pool and a female subject pool separately. This not only excludes, for the moment, any possible contamination resulting from the inclusion of different-sex choices, but also creates the possibility for different treatments of subject selection within an overall similarity of design. In contrast to previous experiments, a study of this type requires that one should be able to draw on a body of subjects within which *no* friendships have yet formed but where there is a plausible basis for the expectation that they will do so. In a university population, such as was available for study, powerful situational determinants of the range of friendship choices would appear to be place of residence and academic subject studied (Warr, 1965) and in view of the intention to use different methods of subject selection, the studies were conducted in two separate Halls of Residence. The require-ments most suited a correlational method (see Chapter 3) and the naturalistic approach of the study obviated any need to engineer interaction. The expectation was that the two situational determinants (same academic subject plus proximity, in one case; close proximity alone in the other) would provide the possibility of mutual involvement in sufficient cases to satisfy the aim of the study (cf. Festinger, Schachter and Back, 1950). However, to minimize the possibility that friendships had already formed, and to begin study right at the start of incipient friendships, subjects were first-year students and took part in the first session of the experiment during the inaugural weeks of their initial term of university life. The studies thus followed the research designs of Izard (1960) and Newcomb (1961) by assessing similarity on two occasions. On the first occasion, similarity between individuals who later became friends was assessed at the very outset of their interaction in a group; on the second occasion it was assessed at a stage when the friendship patterns had been established. This makes it is possible to compare the constructs of friends against those of nominal pairs within the same population prior to acquaintance as well as after a period of continued acquaintance. This fulfils the main aims.

DERIVATION OF SUBJECTS FOR EXPERIMENTS D AND E; AND OVERALL METHODS

It was first necessary to identify two pools of potential subjects and then, confident of their interest in the scientific enterprise, to contact them individually. The criteria of potentiality, which the two experiments required, were that in one case subjects should live in close proximity and that in the other they should follow the same academic course. Large student halls of residence hold a pool of persons in each category by virtue of their physical construction and the character of their intake. Therefore, appropriate groups of students in such residences were approached and their cooperation invited. This resulted in Experiment D being conducted on 12 male students of diverse academic subjects who lived in the same corridor-unit in one hall of residence; and Experiment E having as its subjects 16 female students of Geography who lived *sparsim* in a hall of residence for women. As subjects were in their first year at university, they were minimally acquainted with the other members of their own subject-pool at the time of the first part of the study and were all then in the age range 17–19 years.

In the two cases, the overall method adopted was essentially the same. Subjects were first tested in the first two weeks of their initial academic term at university and were tested a second time 6 months later when the second term of the academic year was in its final weeks. The second test was introduced as one concerned with 'the effects of time upon Reptest performance'. It is likely that this would be the subjects' own inference in any case, as there were no grounds for them to expect the sociometric measures used after the completion of the second Reptest. The reasons for selection of subjects had been kept vague and were given as 'sociological' (i.e. 'study of students in a hall of residence' or 'study of Geography students') and no mention was made during the first test that a second was likely, nor during the second that anything 'extra' was to be accomplished on this occasion. But if there were any 'demand characteristics', it is not clear whether they would be unequivocal. From the subjects' point of view, the alleged rationale of the second test might just as well have pointed to a test of memory of previous responses as it could have been a test of variations from them, and the phrase 'effects of time upon Reptest performance' purposely contains no unambiguous clues. However, it is extremely unlikely that subjects would have made the necessary efforts to remember the constructs once they had completed the first Reptest in view of their unawareness that a second test was to follow in 6 months. For this reason, and the fact that similarities were to be measured between Reptests completed at the same session and not between individuals' responses at sessions One and Two, the effect of this phrase is in no clear direction.

MEASURES AND PROCEDURE FOR EXPERIMENT D

The 12 male subjects were given a form of the Reptest (Kelly, 1955) which had 16 elements and 18 sets of comparison triads. The instructions and element role-titles were as in the previous experiments (see Appendix A) with no requirement for structural measures. This was the only test which the subjects completed at this stage.

Nearly 6 months later the subjects completed a second form of the Reptest of size 12×12. The subjects were reminded of the method of completing the Reptest and were given the first twelve of the role titles used previously, for use in eliciting the constructs in the second test. The size of the Reptest was reduced for this second test to the basic 12 elements (see

Appendix A) and the reduplications of elements were not included here as they had been on the first test. In all other respects the instructions given were the same as in the first part of the study.

When this Reptest had been completed, sociometric techniques were employed to elicit a list of friends. Again, no restriction was placed on the type of person to be included in the friendship list and no limit was made on the numbers to be given, so that there were no instructional demands to name as friends any members of the population under study, although it was hoped that these would be so included in the event.

ANALYSIS OF EXPERIMENT D

Unfortunately, it was clear when the sociometric choice matrix had been compiled, that in this instance the 'naturalistic' stance of the study had been unrewarded and friendship choices between members of the pool were not frequent. It was clear from the matrix that only 4 reciprocated choices had been made (thus implicating a maximum of 8 subjects: in fact, since one subject was involved in two reciprocated choices, the number of such subjects is reduced to 7). Furthermore, some subjects had made no choices within the original pool or had not been chosen by any others in it. One of the major exterior assumptions of the method for deriving subjects (i.e. the assumption that proximity would enhance the possibility that friendships would form within the subject pool) has thus been seriously undermined. However, this appears to support the earlier arguments that proximity is not a sufficient cause of friendship, but that some concept of 'filtering' is a necessary adjunct. The situation therefore provides for a different method of testing the similarity hypothesis, for if no friendships have formed then the filtering-and-similarity hypothesis would predict that there would also be few construct similarities between pairs of subjects. The analysis was therefore carried out as below, following the same basic pattern as that in Chapter 6 (p. 61). Constructs were first compared for similarities according to previously described methods and comparison of the constructs of each subject with those of each other member of the pool were made separately for both sets of Reptests.

However, a methodological change was incorporated into this analysis since 'early' levels of friendship were, at one point, being studied in a natural situation. At the early stages of friendship formation, filtering theory would predict that when construct similarity begins to operate as a filter, the first concern would be with literal similarity since this is the more obvious and easy to discover. Acquainted individuals would find that similarity of words is more easily detected than is any similarity of concepts which may be hidden beneath different words. The awareness of literal similarity would thus facilitate an individual's inference (which may or may not prove to be correct) that similarity of processes is present and this expectation would in no way operate to decrease the likelihood of desire for further interaction (see Chapter 3). However, it may be argued that this concern with the literal content of a system may impose too teasing a constraint on one's comprehension of another's processes. One's notion of 'what he is up to' must depend on some overall grasp of his psychology rather than an exhaustive catalogue of his vocabulary and articulation. A reasonable refinement of the present position would suggest an early dependence on literal similarity but that the *subsequent* emphases in relationships would revolve around the establishment of conceptual similarity (i.e. a broadening of the boundaries of that which counts as similar, to include also ways of expressing the same idea in different words—see Chapter 6, p. 61). By investigating such similarities one could gain a finer insight into the degree of overlap which existed between two systems. In view of this it was felt that the conceptual criterion used previously (Chapter 6) may possibly prove to be too broad and imprecise a measure of the factors which prevail in 'early' acquaintance. A new and more rigorous criterion for similarity was therefore adopted as an additional measure and was termed 'literal similarity'. Two constructs were counted 'literally similar' when exactly the same words were used in each, in the same sense. To ensure that the same sense *was* intended, more frequent analysis of the 'contrast' poles of constructs was necessary, for this gives a clearer insight into the use of the similarity pole (see Chapter 2, p. 18). Thus, if a subject had used the construct 'Fair–Dark' and another subject had used 'Fair–Dark' or 'Fair-Has brown hair', these constructs were counted as similar on the literal criterion, but neither construct was classified similar to 'Fair–Dishonest'. In cases of doubt (e.g. 'Fair–Not fair') the constructs were counted as dissimilar. Interrater reliabilities for literal similarity gave $W = 0.787$, $p < 0.01$. Literal similarity thus embraces an exclusive category of constructs, while conceptual similarity embraces those in the literal category, *plus* instances where a subject used different words to express the same idea, as in the previous analyses (see Chapter 6). Construct similarity between each possible pairing within the subject pool was then assessed for each of the two sets of Reptests independently (i.e. Reptest One similarity scores were assessed and kept separate from those for Reptest Two—there was no cumulation). Similarity was assessed on each of the two criteria separately and the scores thus obtained were then classified according to whether the pairs had chosen each other on the sociometric test ('friendship pairs') or not ('nominal pairs').

For each subject it was thus possible to derive a mean similarity score for all his friendship pairings as had been done previously (Chapter 6, p. 61) and to compare this with the similarity score for all nominal pairs of which he was a member. In order to enliven this procedure, it was completed in each of the following categories:

Literal similarity: Reptest One (1)
                         Reptest Two (2)
Conceptual similarity: Reptest One (3)
                         Reptest Two (4).

Differences between the mean similarity scores derived from friendship pairs and from nominal pairs for each subject were derived by means of Student's *t*-test for the paired case.

In view of the fact that just under half of the subject pool had not been involved in any of the mutual choices made, an additional set of analyses was performed in this experiment only, after the analysis of the complete data described above. The scores of the subjects who had made the mutual choices on the sociometric test were extracted and these 7 sets of scores in each of the above 4 categories were re-analysed independently of the other subjects' scores (except where these other subjects constituted the other half of a nominal pairing for a given subject).

RESULTS AND DISCUSSION OF EXPERIMENT D

The prediction from the filter theory was that (since friendships had not formed to any appreciable degree) there would be little resultant discovery of similarity between pairs of subjects. Inspection of Table 7.1 reveals that none of the tests carried out in this light reached a level of significance and the prediction is thus borne out. This further suggests the inefficacy of proximity as a sufficient condition for friendship and supports the basic contentions of filter theory.

In view of this, if one concentrates on the subjects who did go on to form friendships within the population under study, then some form of construct similarity is predicted by the theory as a characteristic of friendship pairs. However, in testing this contention one reduces the pool to 7 subjects and this approaches the lower limits of statistical viability. Nevertheless, inspection of Table 7.2 indicates that in the sub-analysis of this experiment, one of the *t*-test analyses reached significance. This is evidence of construct similarity between pairs of friends, in category (4). All other results were non-significant.

No great confidence can be placed in these latter results in view of the statistical problems enshrouding them. But even so, the significant result in the sub-analysis and the non-significant results in the main analysis do nothing to undermine the theory of filters. Indeed, the finding in the sub-analysis that conceptual similarity between friends is apparent by the

Table 7.1. Experiment D. (Main analysis)
Differences between the Mean Similarity scores derived from
Friendship and Nominal Pairs

		All constructs
Literal similarity	First Reptest	$\overline{X}_\mathrm{D} = 0 \cdot 1183$ $SD\overline{X}_\mathrm{D} = 1 \cdot 2039$ $t = 0 \cdot 3404$
	Second Reptest	$\overline{X}_\mathrm{D} = 0 \cdot 0325$ $SD\overline{X}_\mathrm{D} = 0 \cdot 6513$ $t = 0 \cdot 1728$
Concept similarity	First Reptest	$\overline{X}_\mathrm{D} = 0 \cdot 4291$ $SD\overline{X}_\mathrm{D} = 1 \cdot 9352$ $t = 0 \cdot 7682$
	Second Reptest	$\overline{X}_\mathrm{D} = 0 \cdot 3375$ $SD\overline{X}_\mathrm{D} = 1 \cdot 0317$ $t = 1 \cdot 1332$

All results NS, $df = 11$.

Table 7.2. Experiment D (Sub-analysis)
Differences between the Mean Similarity scores derived from
the Friendship and Nominal pairing of subjects who formed
friendships

		All constructs
Literal similarity	First Reptest	$\overline{X}_\mathrm{D} = 0 \cdot 5928$ $SD\overline{X}_\mathrm{D} = 1 \cdot 3875$ $t = 1 \cdot 1304$
	Second Reptest	$\overline{X}_\mathrm{D} = 0 \cdot 3000$ $SD\overline{X}_\mathrm{D} = 0 \cdot 7393$ $t = 1 \cdot 0737$
Concept similarity	First Reptest	$\overline{X}d = 1 \cdot 2914$ $SD\overline{X}_\mathrm{D} = 2 \cdot 1342$ $t = 1 \cdot 6010$
	Second Reptest	$\overline{X}_\mathrm{D} = 0 \cdot 9385$ $SD\overline{X}_\mathrm{D} = 0 \cdot 9574$ $t = 2 \cdot 5939*$

* $p < 0 \cdot 05$. $df = 6$.
All other results NS, $df = 6$.

time of the second Reptest is (albeit half-hearted) support for the contention presented earlier: that it is possible that there are changes in the *type* of similarity as a relationship continues.

These results cannot be regarded as conclusive support for the theory, since they fail to provide evidence of the 'A implies B' variety (friendship implies similarity, and vice versa). They merely suggest that 'not-A implies not-B' (non-occurrence of friendship implies non-discovery of similarity, and vice versa). They are thus relegated to the infamous, but familiar, status of 'interesting and suggestive results which are not, however, conclusive. More needs to be done . . .'. More was done, in this instance, and more convincing evidence was discovered in the analysis of Experiment E described below, where a larger number of friendships did develop in the population under study.

MEASURES AND PROCEDURE FOR EXPERIMENT E*

The subjects for this study were 16 girls aged between 17 and 19 years, who were all students of Geography who lived in the same hall of residence and who had been selected provisionally as described in the 'Derivation of Subjects . . .' section above (see p. 76). This study was conducted in a manner identical to Experiment D above, with the following exceptions. The Reptest which subjects completed was a slightly smaller (16 × 16) version of the test, and the elements are listed in Appendix A (a). On the second occasion, nearly 6 months later, subjects completed a comparable 12 × 12 Reptest which represented a reduced version of the first test, using as elements those contained in Appendix A (b). Thus, subjects completed Reptests of different sizes on the two occasions, as had subjects in Experiment D.

In all other respects, the measures and procedure were identical with that previously described for Experiment D.

ANALYSIS OF EXPERIMENT E

Analysis of the sociometric data for this experiment revealed that a far greater number of friendships had developed within the original subject pool during the period between the two tests than was the case in Experiment D, and almost all of the subjects had formed at least two reciprocated friendships within the pool. This provided for a cheerful hope and also

* A different form of this report has previously appeared in: Duck, S. W., and Spencer, C. P., 'Personal constructs and friendship formation', *Journal of Personality and Social Psychology*, **23**, 1972, 40–45.

offered good grounds for the test of the prediction that initial filtering processes would make way for the search for construct similarity, which should therefore be apparent between pairs of friends.

The main analysis of this study echoed the main analysis of Experiment D (p. 78), but it was not necessary on this occasion to perform a 'kiss-of-life' sub-analysis. Table 7.3 shows the significant differences between friendship and nominal pairs for this experiment. Pairs who later became friends have, overall, more similar constructs than nominal pairs on the first Reptest, when similarity is assessed according to the rigorous literal criterion ($p<0.05$), as predicted by the filtering theory, though not when the criterion taken is conceptual similarity. However, after nearly 6 months of acquaintance, the *overall* similarity between friends is no longer significantly greater than that between nominal pairs on either criterion.

Table 7.3. Differences between the Mean Similarity scores derived from Friendship and Nominal pairs

	Similarity criterion		All constructs	Psychological constructs
Literal	First Reptest	Friendship	3·2477	1·3777
		Nominal	2·5096	1·2311
		M_{diff}	0·7381	0·1466
		SD_M	1·2435	0·5065
		t	2·3748*	1·1579
	Second Reptest	Friendship	2·0083	1·3610
		Nominal	1·7340	1·1904
		M_{diff}	0·2743	0·1706
		SD_M	0·9115	0·2758
		t	1·2036	2·4760*
Concept	First Reptest	Friendship	3·9680	1·8199
		Nominal	3·2337	1·5258
		M_{diff}	0·7343	0·2941
		SD_M	1·6286	0·9529
		t	1·8037	1·2346
	Second Reptest	Friendship	2·6139	1·6678
		Nominal	2·1309	1·3175
		M_{diff}	0·4830	0·3503
		SD_M	1·0731	0·5209
		t	1·8008	2·6904**

Note: df = 15 in all cases, all tests are two-tailed.
 * $p < 0.05$.
** $p < 0.025$.

From: Duck, S. W., and Spencer, C. P. (1972). 'Personal constructs and friendship formation,' *Journal of Personality and Social Psychology.* **23**, pp. 40–45.
Copyright 1972 by the American Psychological Association, and reproduced by permission.

This is, at first sight, both puzzling and irritating for it appears that the possibility of changes in similarity has submerged itself. But what if there is a parallel process to that suggested? What if one of the proposals of Chapter 1 has actually manifested itself in concrete form? In parallel to the possibility that concern changes from literal to conceptual (p. 79, the arguments of Chapters 1 and 4 (especially those on 'psychological description') would suggest a concentration on the more specific constructs within a system. These arguments propose an attention to those constructs which describe other people at the level of character, personality and psychological characteristics. Such descriptions were argued in Chapter 1 to be sources of validational doubts and to be especially the kind of description on which a social comparison and social reality grounding would be valuable. However, in view of the complex and personal nature of these constructs one would wish only to compare oneself with, and gain validity from, those with whom one felt some commonality or for whom one felt respect (cf. a parallel argument, with empirical support, in Festinger, 1954). Thus filter theory would not predict an emphasis on such constructs until after the development of friendship to a stage beyond the primitive. In other words, a concern for psychological construing should be evident (and should be evident only) after friendship had become firmer. In terms of the present measures, this predicts that a concern for psychological construing should manifest itself on the second Reptest and that similarity on this kind of construct should distinguish friendship pairs.

Such a possibility has plainly exciting implications for the development of filter theory and, as a measure of it, a classification of constructs was used (after Bieri, Bradburn and Galinsky, 1958; and B. R. Little, personal communication). This entailed the scrutiny of each construct and its subsequent assignment to one of the three following exclusive and exhaustive categories: psychological, role, other. (A further category was devised later and is described in the next chapter.) *Psychological* constructs were those describing a character, personality or cognitive attribute of an individual: e.g. 'Ambitious—Not ambitious', 'Self-opinionated and moody—More consistent', 'Helpful and kindly nature–Selfish and bitchy'. The constructs assigned to the *Role* category were those which described habitual activities or roles: e.g. 'Sing and play guitar–Can't do either', 'Male–Female', 'Teachers–Personnel manager'. *Other* constructs were those which were not clearly assignable to the above two categories, or those where the ingenuity of the construer was beyond that of the experimenter: e.g. 'Both stand a chance–No chance at all', 'Lusty–Looks impotent', 'Room-mates, young and in love–Can't imagine him in love'. The interrater reliability for assigning constructs to categories was measured by χ^2 and gave $\chi^2 = 242 \cdot 71$, $df = 4$, $p < 0 \cdot 001$.

Armed with this categorization of constructs it was possible to separate the psychological constructs and treat them separately in order to test certain of the predictions of filter theory. The first of these proclaimed increases both in psychological construing itself and in the revelation of it to others, as relationships developed. Some changes in construing with time are predicted by PCT (Personal Construct Theory) also and this was one of the main reasons for its adoption. Between the first and second Reptests there was an increase in the percentage of psychological constructs used by subjects from 26·6 per cent to 35·6 per cent (pooled data). More importantly, the main prediction is also supported. For although after nearly 6 months of acquaintance, the *overall* similarity between friends is no longer significantly greater than between nominal pairs, when one looks only at the psychological constructs friendship pairs are significantly more alike than nominal pairs, whether the criterion for similarity is literal ($p < 0.05$) or conceptual ($p < 0.02$), as Table 7.3 shows.* A shift in the kinds of similarity which matter is suggested.

However, some might wish to argue as follows: 'During the course of the study and its intervening period, all subjects came to use proportionately more psychological constructs than they had done on the first test. Can it be clarified whether the significant similarities among psychological constructs simply arise from this or do they really operationalize a change in the value and relevance of construct types during friendship's progressive development?' An answer to this line of thought is evident in Table 7.4. This shows that there are decreases in the absolute amounts of similarity within friendship pairs and within nominal pairs when a comparison is made between the first and second Reptests over all constructs (i.e. before separation of the psychological constructs). Such a fall in similarity levels may reflect a diversification of construct labels as a result of 6 months of university training (Izard, 1963), which may cause smaller consequent amounts of overlap between the systems as a whole. This pattern recurs in the case of psychological constructs on their own, but the result is not significant. It should be observed that the decrease in similarities in the case of friendship pairs is absolutely smaller than for nominal pairs and the changes *within* pairings are enough to create the significant differences revealed *between* nominal pairs and friendship pairs (Table 7.3). This is evidence that those similarities between psychological constructs which are evident at this stage of friendship are increasingly the similarities which most strongly differentiate the friendship pairs from the nominal pairs.

* It is clearly a complete waste of time to re-analyse the main data from Experiment D with this new classification system, if the hypothesis here is correct. This is because the reason for paring off the psychological constructs rests on the formation and development of friendships. However, to silence the sceptics, this fruitless task was undertaken nevertheless and all results, as predicted, were non-significant.

Table 7.4. A comparison of the Mean Similarity scores obtained in the two Reptests (R1 and R2)

Constructs considered			Nominal pairs	Friendship pairs
All	Literal	R1	2·5096	3·2477
		R2	1·7340	2·0083
		M_{diff}	0·7756	1·2394
		SD_M	0·7695	1·3001
		t	4·0332**	3·8135**
	Concept	R1	3·2337	3·9680
		R2	2·1309	2·6139
		M_{diff}	1·1028	1·3541
		SD_M	0·7563	1·4985
		t	5·5047***	3·6147*
Psychological	Literal	R1	1·2311	1·3777
		R2	1·1904	1·3610
		M_{diff}	0·0407	0·0167
		SD_M	0·2381	0·5603
		t	0·6840	0·1192
	Concept	R1	1·5258	1·8199
		R2	1·3175	1·6678
		M_{diff}	0·2083	0·1521
		SD_M	0·4103	0·9122
		t	2·0321	0·6671

Note: $df = 15$ in all cases, all test are two-tailed.

 * $p < 0.01$.

 ** $p < 0.002$.

*** $p < 0.001$.

From: Duck, S. W., and Spencer, C. P. (1972). 'Personal constructs and friendship formation,' *Journal of Personality and Social Psychology*, **23**, pp. 40–45.

Copyright 1972 by the American Psychological Association, and reproduced by permission.

RESULTS FROM FURTHER ANALYSIS COMPARING EXPERIMENTS D AND E

In order to put Experiment E in its proper perspective, further analysis was performed to effect a comparison with Experiment D. There are perhaps incidental factors which could have contributed to the observation of low levels of friendship in Experiment D. For example, the diffusion of academic courses followed may have provided some subjective filters, for only two subjects shared a common academic course. It could be argued (as a parallel to, and as a sub-class division of, the hypotheses of Bernstein, 1958, and Whorf, 1956) that academic subject studied may reflect something of the thought processes manifest in individuals, in the way that class differences are apparent in construing (Warren, 1966). This possibility will be reconsidered in another light in Chapter 12, where it may be seen to have wider implications.

In this instance it is important for filter theory to note the low number of similarities recorded in any category of Experiment D, before their classification into those derived from friendship and those from nominal pairs, since the relationship between similarity and friendship is the central hypothesis. A comparison of this relationship in the different populations of study revealed the following significant differences.

Similarity scores generated by pairing each subject in turn with all other subjects from his own subject-pool had already been derived. These original scores, before subsequent classification, were now used to derive for each subject a mean similarity score which represented the amount of similarity which he showed, on average, to another subject in his pool. Such means were also derived from subjects in the second subject pool and overall comparison of the two sets of means showed highly significant differences in all categories tested (*First test*: literal similarity: $t = 4·322$, $df = 26$, $p < 0·001$; concept similarity: $t = 5·677$, $df = 26$, $p < 0·001$; *Second test*: literal similarity: $t = 3·487$, $df = 26$, $p < 0·002$; concept similarity: $t = 4·117$, $df = 26$, $p < 0·001$). This indicates that the average amount of construct similarity between subjects in the male group was highly significantly lower than the average amounts between subjects in the female group. In terms of the present hypothesis this means that the ground for friendship formation was also significantly less. On this basis the present view would also predict that a significant difference should be found between the absolute number of mutual choices made by each subject in the two groups, as an indicator of the relative amounts of friendship choice within the two subject pools. The two sets of scores were indeed found to be significantly different, with significantly fewer friendship choices made by the male subjects than were made by the female subjects ($t = 6·131$, $df = 26$, $p < 0·001$).

Thus, comparison of the two studies shows that the one where significantly lower amounts of construct similarity were found between the members of its subject pool also manifests significantly lower amounts of friendship choice within that pool. These results were predicted from the filtering–similarity hypothesis.

DISCUSSION OF THE COMPARISON OF THE TWO EXPERIMENTS

These latter two studies were intended to exemplify certain methodological and subjective differences which were of significance to the development of filter theory. One difference from other studies was the concentration on subjects choosing from within a single-sex subject pool; the difference between the studies lay in the sex of the subject pool and in the exterior forces which were expected to facilitate the development of friendships. The comparison of the two studies has shown the interest of these questions to differing extents.

There was no clear disclosure of consistent differences of strategy within populations of same-sex friends, as a parallel to the claims of Chapter 6 that such differences were apparent in a different-sex subject pool where cross-sex choices were expressed. The findings here were again that, where friendship developed, they were related to amounts of construct similarity. The fact that same-sex choices are based on similar strategies in both sexes supports the claims of Chapter 6 and points to the important fact that established 'friendship' has been shown to have a further complexity previously undisclosed for its basis may differ depending on whether cross-sex or same-sex choices are reviewed. The implication of this is that the deeper personal relations with people of the same sex may reflect a different level of relationship from that manifested in cross-sex choices (as in marital partnerships). This intriguing possibility remains for further comment later (Chapters 11 and 12). But as well as 'real-life' relevance, such a claim also has a centrality in those ivory towers where the resolution of complementarity and similarity hypotheses is of importance. Some of the discrepancy between the successes of the two may be seen to be due to the types of partnership on which such hypotheses were tested. These implications will be further discussed later in the light of subsequent evidence.

The second result of the comparison of these two studies indicates the relative powers of different situational determinants of attraction. Proximity on its own (even proximity in a corridor-unit, where all facilities were shared) seems not to be a sufficient determinant of attraction if the academic subjects of the students involved are allowed to reflect the wide spectrum of possibilities. It is frequently claimed by allocators of student rooms that as wide as possible a range of subjects should be represented in each living unit in order to provide students with the possibility of sampling the techniques and problems of other disciplines by discussion with its trainees. By such means it is hoped to add a further dimension to the breadth of education which students may acquire in a university. The evidence of this single study on male students appears to suggest that this claim should be treated cautiously, for it seems that proximity on its own may not be a sufficient cause of friendship (and therefore one would expect that it may not be a sufficient cause of interactions of the type which increases familiarity with other subjects. It seems, therefore, that it may not be a sufficient cause of the intercourse which it was argued to promote, with its subsequent benefits).

On the other hand, female students of the same academic subject would appear to develop stronger ties within the pool of others from their own course, if they meet on the informal basis which common dwelling provides as well as on the more formal opportunities provided by lectures and other academic occasions. Therefore it is obvious that the above claims require tempering by the consideration of further aspects which are of relevance ('alphabetical' selection has already been pointed out, p. 64. Clearly, opportunities for interaction must further be increased by common sporting or recreational activities, for example. One might expect that the effects of mere proximity could be alleviated by such factors.

The comparison of the two studies does therefore raise some interesting speculation on the sociological and demographic implications of this work. These implications have been argued to rest on the possible differences in cognitive processes which may occur in sub-classes of a given population. These aspects of friendship make clear further possible relations between the submerged influences of thought processes on social interactions, and while some of the ramifications lie outside the purview of the present programme they clearly represent topics of urgent relevance to a complete understanding of the phenomena of interpersonal attraction—a further testimony to the claim that the complexity of the topic should not be underestimated.

DISCUSSION OF EXPERIMENT E

While Experiment D supported the filter hypothesis by showing that where there were few similarities of constructs there were few consequent friendships; Experiment E has contended more strongly for the theory by showing that where there were higher levels of similarity there were more friendships. That similarity of constructs is a precursor of friendship and not simply its product is shown by the similarity between eventual friends, found in the first Reptest before these friendships had occasion to form. Inevitably this bald statement is a trifle too simple. The picture is complicated by two other elements: the changes in the kind of similarity which are important; and the possible normative influences which result from group membership. It is evident from Table 7.3 that the types of similarity which are manifested at different stages of the acquaintance process are themselves different in kind. In the early stages it is literal similarity of constructs of all types which differentiates friendship pairs from nominal pairs; in later stages the similarity which is important is similarity of psychological constructs. Clearly this allows the possibility that similarity serves a different function at the two stages; this suggests that the type of similarity which is manifest at the early levels is a precursor of friendship because of what it *suggests* rather than because of what it *is*. In other words, 'literal' similarity may be relevant at an early stage of friendship because it suggests 'psychological' similarity. This suggestion may be tested in subsequent interactions. Such a proposal goes a lot further than the present results warrant. It also goes a lot further than some current approaches to friendship and attraction (Berscheid and Walster, 1969; Murstein, 1972) and it clearly invites empirical support. The next two chapters will examine some of its ramifications.

The above discussion of one complication to the statement that similarity is a precursor of friendship should not be allowed to overshadow a second complexity. The normative effects of group membership are well known (e.g. Thibaut and Kelley, 1959) and it may be that normative effects are responsible for some of the specific changes of particular constructs which occur over time. This, of course, is a different claim from the proposition that *types* (rather than specific instances) of constructs change with the development of friendship. The changes in specific constructs may result from common assessments of others and, within an overall shift to psychological construing, specific agreements on the psychological assessment of others would inexorably result in similarities becoming apparent. However, the present position perforce takes the view that such similarities as result from friendship must be regarded as subsidiary to and vastly fewer than the number of similarities which precede friendship. Otherwise, the prediction whose fulfilment has been demonstrated in these experiments would lose its theoretical basis.

Such considerations invoke a corollary to filter theory: namely that filtering continues after the search for similarity begins and similarity, of itself, is not a sufficient condition for friendship. The similarity sought is similarity of the highest level of construing, and the hypothesis here advanced is that early construing of others, and the process of filtering in general, must involve the further process of extrapolating from one's construal of another person to an hypothesis about what his constructs may be. As these extrapolations are confirmed or disconfirmed, so the process continues to shift upwards to what his 'higher order' constructs may be. The discovery (and continued affirmation) of actual similarity between these higher order constructs and one's own is a sufficient condition for the formation (and continuation) of friendship.

CONCLUSIONS

Such considerations as the above begin to bring us closer to person perception and to a vindication of the earlier claims that person perception and friendship formation are related, if not identical. They have also provided a further emphasis for the programme of research. But while cast in general terms above, they can be put into a more concrete form for investigation. In functional terms, the hypothesis implies that at the early stages of interaction an individual in a new group uses constructs about manner and physical attractiveness, for example, in assessing his new acquaintances. Only later do the individual's other constructs become more salient; and he progresses to guessing the range of the other person's construct system and hypothesizing the amount of overlap which he may find later to exist between that system and his own. B. R. Little (personal communication) has argued that ontological development proceeds through the stages of physicalistic to role construing and then to psychological construing. The longitudinal study of the development of friendship may provide a parallel to his process.

These suggestions indicate clearly different stages through which an individual is hypothesized to pass before accepting a person to be a 'potential friend': the first amounts to concern with the non-psychological construing of the other person (in crude terms) and the second to an hypothesis about the character which deeper levels of constructs may reveal themselves to have. In the first case, filtering by evaluation and assessment of interaction styles will lead to a continued willingness to interact, which can become firmly established friendship if the deeper roots of construction processes are seen to be similar to one another.

The empirical question thus becomes: 'Given that PCT methods can distinguish friendship pairs from nominal pairs at the stages of friendship so far studied, by pointing out similarities between friends, what are the qualitative differences which it can reveal to clarify the processes involved?'. Put into other words, the question is functionalized as: 'To what extent do subjects describe new acquaintances in different terms from well-known acquaintances, when tested by the methods derived from PCT?'

8

Stages of Acquaintance

The argument has been that as interaction continues, and as the friend-ship between individuals increases, there is a shift from describing one another in terms of role or physical constructs to descriptions more heavily loaded with psychological import. It follows from this that investigation of the early stages of acquaintance in more depth should reveal that subjects are less prone to describe newly-met individuals in terms of underlying 'motivation' than to describe them in physical or role terms. It cannot at this stage be clarified whether these types of description are felt by subjects to be important at this level of interaction, or whether greater emphasis is placed on them because they are felt to be the only type of description available. Clearly, in the literal sense, they are *not* the only type of descrip-tion available. Subjects can still presumably use their psychologically de-scriptive labels, but to do so would be more inferential, less tied to evidence which is plainly and unambiguously categorizable (such as evidence on height, hair colour, etc.), and less easy, at this stage, to validate since (except in certain circumstances—e.g. interviews) such evidence is not a normal major outcome of interaction at such a level. However, it is clear that the focus of attention is increasingly shifting towards the 'area' of person percep-tion where evidence shows that subjects are prepared to make inferences from small pieces of information (Thornton, 1944, who showed the effects of spectacles on impressions of deeper characteristics; McKeachie, 1952, who did the same with lipstick; Kramer, 1963, on non-verbal information; Miller, 1970, with physical characteristics). It has already been claimed in Chapters 1 and 4 that such inferences can be far-reaching (e.g. De Charms et al., 1965; Briscoe et al., 1967, have already been described). So it is a valid inference from this area that these early interactions, based on very superficial evidence, are not without their evaluative outcomes, even if the constructs used to describe them and their participants may appear trivial.

The need, then, is for an investigation of what happens very early in acquaintance and the present study provides a means of finding out those constructs which are used by subjects to describe people whom they have just met. The use to which they put such information and the inferences drawn from it will not be studied here and the whole question is sufficiently complex to require its own investigation, reported in the next chapter. At this point one is interested solely in discovering the differences which there are in descriptions of new acquaintances from those applied to well-known associates. The hypothesis of filtering is clearly that subjects will concentrate less on 'psychological construing' than on mundane construing of physical characteristics and other lower level filters, even though the higher orders of construing are still available to them.

METHOD FOR EXPERIMENT F

The requirements of the experiment necessitated using subjects who did not know one another and providing them with information on other subjects who could then be used as elements in the Reptest. Tests thus completed could be compared with tests derived from construing of intimate associates to offer some clarification of the differences between the two situations in PCT terms.

Accordingly, the earlier technique was adopted of using first-year students as subjects and conducting the experiment during the first week of their first term, to facilitate the inference that subjects were not acquainted with one another, except in any superficial sense. In this instance, the experiment was conducted at the Sheffield Polytechnic, by arrangement with the Liaison Officer. Thirty-seven subjects constituted the subject-pool for this experiment, all aged in the range 17 to 19 years, and of this number, 14 were female and 23 male.

The experiment was introduced as one intended to investigate the way in which people categorize others and subjects were given the 16×18 form of the Reptest as a measure of this. Instructions and role-titles to elicit elements were standard (Appendix A). All role-titles on this first test were thus designed to elicit more intimate acquaintances as elements. When this Reptest had been completed, it was necessary to divide the subject pool into smaller groups, as below.

In order to give subjects some new acquaintances with whom they could interact in a new situation where all would participate, subjects were assigned to discussion groups which were to consider the problems on a Kogan and Wallach (1964) Choice-Dilemmas Questionnaire* and reach

* In these problems some fictitious individual is faced with a decision between a 'safe' but less-attractive prospect, and a 'risky' but very attractive prospect. For example, a man with a heart disease must choose between a routine operation which will leave him partially incapacitated and a very risky operation which, if successful, would enable him to resume an active life. The task of the subjects in this situation is to 'advise' the individual on what action he should choose, or more precisely, they must decide on the lowest probability of success in the 'risky' venture which they would be prepared to countenance as acceptable.

unanimous decisions. There were 4 groups of 7 persons and 1 of 9 members, and the groups were constructed with the intention of eliminating any possibility of known germinal friendship pairs being included in the same group. It was thus contrived that people who had chosen to sit next to one another for the first test were assigned to different groups. Each group was composed of subjects who did not know one another, and the ultimate success of the manipulation was verified during the subsequent debriefing. The difference in sex ratios was balanced as far as was possible (i.e. one group contained 3 females and 4 males; another was composed of 4 females and 3 males; one of 7 males and another of 7 females; and the large group consisted of 9 males). Each member of all groups was given a duplicated sheet containing the Kogan and Wallach problems and the groups were sent to separate rooms to conduct their discussions. No experimenter was present with any group during their deliberations, except insofar as it was necessary from time to time to divine the progress being made. When they had finished, and before the groups were disassembled, the members of each group were told the importance of remembering the names, faces or some such feature of the other members for the next part of the experiment.

The task-oriented nature of these groups would seem to represent the lowest level of group in which strangers meet for short discussion and is thus intermediate between 'groups' where members do not interact at all (see Chapter 10, p. 112) and those where they may interact socially, without a task to perform. The instruction to come to unanimous decisions is likely to ensure (perhaps minimal) contributions from all group members and the design of the experiment (Reptest—discussion—the expectation of another task) was intended to appear transparent. In other words, it was hoped to awaken subjects to the prospect of construing group members. This is seen as casting the experiment against the hypothesis, thus making a confirmation more valuable, for the reason that it may encourage 'normal construing' rather than showing any overriding effects due to the earliness of the acquaintance process being studied here. If a change from the normal is observed then it must be due to a difference in the value of the kinds of construing, since the process of discussion (on such emotive issues as the Kogan and Wallach problems) allows for the formation of constructs about a person's deeper attributes. For discussion of Choice-Dilemma problems involves more everyday processes and exposes more of individuals' personal opinions, values, 'sympathetic orientation' and psychological characteristics than do other possible group tasks (e.g. group solving of creativity problems—Freedman, Klevansky and Ehrlich, 1971; or group planning of a 'living-learning' dormitory—Aronoff and Messé, 1971).

When all groups had completed all the problems on the sheet (i.e. after about 40 minutes), subjects were re-assembled in the main experimental room and given a further 16 × 18 form of the Reptest. The elements were the 7 (or in the case of the large group, any 7) members of the discussion group of which a subject was a member. This included 'self'. With 7 elements and 16 element-spaces, repetition of the elements in the test was possible so that a large number of comparisons could be elicited. The elements were arranged thus: the first 6 elements were the members of the group apart from self; the element used first was repeated as the 7th element; the 8th and 9th elements were 'self'; and for the next 7 elements, repetition was made (in this order) of the elements already used in positions 6,4,2,1,3,5 and 8. This method enabled production of several permutations of comparison triads from the same pool of subject-elements and was thus very germane in a study of this sort where the maximum number of descriptions of group members is the ideal.

When subjects had completed this section of the study, they were thanked for their cooperation and paid for taking part.

The design of this experiment deliberately included no counterbalancing and this approach was taken for two reasons. First, it was manifestly impossible for subjects to use as elements members of a discussion group which had never been convened and so this would have meant some subjects beginning the experiment with a discussion group and then completing 2 Reptests one after the other. From the subjects' point of view, this method would have been entirely unacceptable; and from the experimenter's point of view there was a not unreasonable fear that the fatigue involved would have generated artefacts. Secondly, the present design of the experiment clearly leans *against* the experimental hypothesis in that it gives practice in 'normal' construing, by allowing subjects to construe well-known others (thus providing an empirical baseline for the least artificial situation) before they describe the others in their group. Thus, any results showing that they do not, in the event, use 'normal' proportions of the types of constructs to apply to their group-companions are all the more indicative of differences between normal description and description of those who have just been met for the first time. As such, any result of this kind would be most important for the hypothesis, since it suggests the operation of filters and evaluation.

ANALYSIS AND RESULTS

There were no sociometric data for analysis in this experiment, since the study was concerned with the investigation of acquaintance at its very beginning, before friendship patterns had emerged. The analysis therefore concentrated on the question of differences between the types of constructs used in the 2 tests. Furthermore the decisions taken by the groups on the Kogan and Wallach problems were not investigated here either. The data from the discussion groups were incidental to the main purpose of the experiment, since the groups had been formed only to allow subjects to interact with a small selection of other subjects. The charge given to the groups was to come to unanimous decisions on each problem and the nature of the task makes it mandatory for some minimal contribution to be made by each and every member of the group. Therefore some basis was provided for each subject to gather information on all the other members of his group. The questions which can be asked in the analysis of such situations as this are two-fold: 'What sort of information is it which subjects gather?' and also 'What use is made of the information that is gathered?' However, at this stage, the design of the experiment was created to answer the first question only. It is logically prior to the second and quite distinct from it. The latter requires a more sophisticated and intricate design such as those described in Chapters 9 and 10 where the second question is attacked.

The constructs supplied by all subjects in both parts of the experiment were each rated into one of the three categories: 'psychological', 'role' or 'other', as in Chapter 7. Three independent raters achieved a reliability for assigning constructs to categories here (on the Binomial Test) of $z = 9 \cdot 167$, $p < 0 \cdot 001$. This analysis was done 'blind', to eliminate raters' knowledge of which part of the experiment had produced each Reptest which they were rating. When the constructs on all Reptests had been rated into one of these categories, a comparison was made of the proportions of each type of construct used in the 2 tests.

The results indicated significantly lower uses of psychological constructs in the second Reptest when considering others who had just met ($t = 7 \cdot 67$, $df = 36$, $p < 0.001$). There was a corresponding significant increase in 'role construing' ($t = 6 \cdot 12$, $df = 36$, $p < 0 \cdot 001$). This shows contrasts between the types of information used when describing an intimate acquaintance from that used to describe someone who had just been encountered. When the Reptests of the two sexes were analysed separately, the same picture emerged as had done in the general analysis ($t = 5 \cdot 12$, $df = 22$, $p < 0 \cdot 001$, for male subjects' psychological constructs; and $t = 6 \cdot 19$, $df = 13$, $p < 0 \cdot 001$, for female subjects'). It is interesting to compare this information with the findings of Chapter 6 that certain sex differences in construing can be divined. From the present result it appears that differences in construing are apparent between the sexes only when studied in a mixed-sex subject pool where individuals are acquainted. In relation to the findings of Chapters 6 and 7, this finding indicates that each sex begins by gathering the same kind of information but goes on, in the cross-sex choices, to make somewhat divergent use of it.

DISCUSSION AND FURTHER ANALYSIS OF EXPERIMENT F

The hypothesis of this study was that in describing new acquaintances, subjects would be less prone to particularize them in terms of underlying 'motivation' and psychological factors; and this hypothesis has been upheld, both when all subjects are considered together and when the data from the the two sexes are taken separately. It may be argued that this is because, for some artefactually induced reason, psychological constructs cease to be available to subjects in this situation, perhaps as a function of the task. However, the evidence is strongly against this view. For despite the fact that subjects had been acquainted with the others in their group for a maximum of 40 minutes, Table 8.1 shows that many subjects still construed their fellow members in psychological terms on occasions, although not to any marked degree. This supports the view that the 'unnatural' distribution of construct types after construing new acquaintances is a reflection of emphases which are subjectively important, rather than artefacts of the situation. For this perhaps demonstrates that it is not because they *could not* do so that subjects generally *did not* use psychological constructs in this context. Clearly such methods are still available, but subjects nevertheless choose to use them to a significantly smaller extent than normal.

However, the study as described so far does not tell us the sort of things with which subjects do concern themselves at this stage. It is evident that they do not concentrate on the psychological aspects and evaluations of others' underlying structure, but the type of constructs which they do rely on lies submerged. There have recently been investigations of similar problems from different viewpoints and the results of those studies in no way conflict with the hypothesis advanced here. The view of Lischeron and La Gaipa (1970) and Canfield and La Gaipa (1970 (a), (b)) is, broadly, that at the early stages of acquaintance subjects concentrate on the physical and interactional aspects of the person. As friendship develops, the personalities of the interactors may assume greater importance. This suggestion closely resembles that presented earlier on the microcosmic reflection of ontology in interaction. This alerts one to further examination of its potential here.

Perhaps it is the case that at the early stage subjects use constructs of an interactionally focused sort. In other words, subjects take note of and apply constructs to others' interaction abilities and styles. This may reflect a fitting of others on to stereotype piles before the individuation that inevitably follows further depth of knowledge. To investigate this possibility, all constructs were re-examined.

An additional category was created and all constructs were reconsidered in this light, with reassignment to the new category if this was more appropriate than the previous categorization. This new fourth category subsumed 'interaction constructs'. Examples of constructs given this title were 'Talkative–Quiet', 'Has a loud voice–Speaks softly', and 'Gesticulates–Restrains his gestures'. Constructs on all Reptests from both the first and second parts of the experiment were examined and an analysis conducted as before on the resulting categorizations as 'Interaction constructs'. It was found that significantly more interaction constructs were used when describing new acquaintances ($t=4\cdot186$, $df=36$, $p<0\cdot001$).

This result fills the gap in the previous analysis and makes clearer the nature of the constructs which assume importance at the very early stages of new interactions.

Table 8.1. A comparison of percentages of construct types under two conditions of construing

Conditions of construing	Construct types			
	Psychological	Role	Interaction	Other
Normal (i.e. construing of well-known others)	63·04	24·43	6·24	6·40
Interaction (i.e. construing of newly met others)	20·34	35·24	37·60	6·73

CONCLUSION

This study presents evidence to support the contention advanced in the previous chapter that there are at least two stages of acquaintance, for it has been shown again, on different criteria, that the phenomena which are of importance early in the acquaintance process may not be the same as those used 'normally' to describe those who are better known. It has been shown here that the early constructs of acquaintances used by individuals are based on the interaction styles of those whom they meet. Earlier evidence suggests that a progression then follows to a search for some form of construct similarity. It appears that the criteria for friendship colour and change with the development of friendship, and that similarity of psychological construing is ultimately discernible between those who enter into friendship with one another.

This position confronts the investigation with two possible hypotheses. Either the stages follow one another in discrete progression, automatically, each entered without the benefit of previous experience; or else evidence from one stage is organized and translated into hypotheses for the next or subsequent stages, where the hypotheses can be tested. The (frequently re-warded) attentive will observe that the latter alternative is framed in the language of filter theory and, inevitably, is therefore the preferred choice. This would suggest that early filters take their meaning and importance from the implications which each piece of evidence is seen to have for higher-order construing. In terms of filter theory, some results of an individual's filtering may give him the feeling that he will prove to be similar to this new-found acquaintance of his, when he gets down to psychological constructs.

If this line of inference is a valid one, then early information may have implications of a psychological nature and this is one of the paths of progression suggested by this study. The first call is for examination of the relationship between early constructs and the use made of them; and the second is for investigation of different types of group (casual, task, social) and a search for the differences of friendship patterns and constructional strategies which are observable as a function of differences in the stages of acquaintance which the experimental manipulation permits. These investigations will be conducted separately and successively.

9

Explorations of the Use Made of Early Construing

Some prelusive investigations into the nature of the constructs used in new affiliative situations have suggested that individuals may make quite considerable use of the apparently mundane data which they collect by means of the constructs used at these early stages. It remains to be seen, however, whether individuals are simply making direct use of the information which they have available or whether this information carries a less superficial significance. The latter view is suggested by the assumptions of the present outlook. Such a perspective is concordant with some of the work on impression formation discussed earlier (e.g. Asch, 1946; Burns, 1964; Warr and Knapper, 1968) and the previous experiment shows that the approach adopted here is able to retain information accessible to the methods in the related 'area' of person perception.

Hinkle (1965, reported in Bannister and Mair, 1968) has elaborated some of the suggestions of Kelly (1955), seeing the implications of the two poles of a construct as running up or down the construct system (i.e. they can be 'subordinate' or 'superordinate' implications). A superordinate construct is one which includes another as one of the elements of its context; and a subordinate construct is one which is included as an element in the context of another. Hinkle argues that 'constructs will be regarded as having only one characteristic, quality, or property; namely, a construct has differential *implications* in a given hierarchical *context*'. Thus the construct 'New–Old' might have the implication 'More reliable–Less reliable' in the context of motor cars; but it would not necessarily carry a similar implication in the context of personal acquaintances. Hinkle argues further that superordinate constructs carry a greater number of implications than subordinate constructs and so the line of implication between subordinate and superordinate constructs is not always reciprocal.

The application of such reasoning to filter theory (and to the comments on stereotypes in the latter chapter) is plain. The context of a construct is supplied in part by the situation where it is used and in part by the associations which it carries. Each construct has implications for the rest of the system. Although this line of argument derives from the structural approach to PCT, it can be continued into the content approach to suggest the following: the constructs used at the early stages of acquaintance, be they ever so humble and based on interaction styles and items describing physical or perhaps simple role characteristics, may nevertheless be subordinate to constructs of a psychological nature. They may therefore carry implications for psychological construing, which offer an individual more possibilities for elaboration, association within the system and inference as to another's 'character', or to the way in which the other person associates and organizes his own constructs within his own system. Such activities and inferences may be distinct from, or prior to, or simultaneous with 'direct' construing of another's psychological attributes; or the emphasis on one type or the other may shift as a function of time. However, the specific suggestion here is that progression through the stages of acquaintance, and the frequency of interaction which it genders, facilitates the use of more superordinate and differentiated constructs by allowing for testing of previously derived hypotheses and extrapolations to those superordinate constructs. This perhaps underlies the process observed by Homans (1950, p. 115): 'You can get to like some pretty queer customers, if you go around with them long enough'; for increased interaction must force recognition of any construct similarity which obtains. Free operation of filtering processes could have obliterated this similarity by causing discontinuation of that which may have been seen (erroneously) at an early stage to be an unfruitful acquaintance. Erroneous extrapolation and superordination could thus create faults in implication derivation and in filtering, which forced-interaction could possibly help to overcome in some cases. Of course, the converse would also be true, that erroneous extrapolation may indicate fruitfulness of acquaintance when further interaction reveals its barrenness.

The view adopted here clearly combines the advantages of cognitive parsimony (since it assumes that fewer constructs are used to subsume large numbers of subordinate 'events') with a greater level of information (since superordinate constructs have more subordinate implications than those few whose observation led to the superordinate construct originally being implicated. For example, 'Wears a suit—Does not wear a suit', 'Smiles a lot–Does not smile a lot', 'Agrees frequently–Less ingratiating' may implicate the superordinate construct 'Ambitious–Not ambitious' which in turn suggests both 'Untrustworthy–Trustworthy', and 'Eats at Berni Inns—Does not'). Such a procedure leads to greater possibilities for testing hypotheses. The present study is intended to operationalize this discussion and test the hypothesis that information attended to earlier is used evaluatively and implicatively, so that the deeper, superordinate constructs of a system can be brought into play before any *direct* evidence on them is present. To this end an analysis can be made of the qualitative differences between constructs elicited by consideration of personally unknown people and the data supplied as implications of these constructs.

Furthermore, the study was intended to amplify the suggestions of the previous experiment by using two sets of elements who were not intimate acquaintances of the subjects. The two sets of elements used were different from each other in status, but neither set contained acquaintances with whom friendships had formed. In one case the elements were distant well-known public figures (e.g. Prince Charles) and the degree of knowledge which subjects had of these elements is comparable with the knowledge afforded in studies of acquaintance where subjects are merely given the attitude profile of 'some other person', who is in fact fictitious (e.g. Byrne and Rhamey, 1965). The second type of elements were individuals whom the subject had encountered in a group on two occasions. The correspondence here is more to studies where others are met in like circumstances (e.g. Hogan and Mankin, 1970), but the study is different from that described in Chapter 8 for the reason that the others had been met incidentally at least twice before the experimental session. The study thus provides for a further differentiation which may be possible between different types of acquaintance classed together in the literature. The study thus offers several simultaneous lines of progression in the testing of the filter theory and in elucidating the stages of acquaintance.

METHOD FOR EXPERIMENT G

Subjects in Experiment G were all introductory students of psychology and were in the age range 17 to 19 years. Of the 62 subjects who took part, 49 were female and in view of the disparity in the representation of the two sexes, no separate comparisons were made of the data deriving from each. Subjects took part in the experiment as a compulsory part of their course.

In view of the didactic nature of the situation which necessitated providing data for the students to discuss and write up themselves, the experiment was designed generally to introduce the area of impression formation and so the specific parts of it which were relevant to this course of studies were embedded within a more general overall structure. Subjects were therefore not apprised of the immediate purpose of the study but were given an outline of its more general purposes. These were introduced as a study of 'first impressions' and a brief initiation into the workings of PCT. (It may be noted that this design is a functional testament to the earlier comments that one act can serve several simultaneous purposes and enjoy membership of several classes!)

On the first occasion of testing, subjects were presented with a list of 5 elements, each of which occurred twice on a 10 × 10 Reptest. These 5 elements were public figures who were expected to be well known to subjects yet beyond the range of their personal acquaintance. They were: Lord Montgomery of Alamein; Bernadette Devlin, M.P.; H.R.H. Prince Charles; Racquel Welch and (inevitably) Malcolm Muggeridge. These elements were used by all subjects. After completion of this Reptest, subjects were asked to take the positive (i.e. similarity) pole of each construct at a time and consider what its implications were. Specifically, they were asked: 'If a person has the quality denoted by the positive pole, what other characteristics is he likely to have?' Subjects were asked to restrict themselves to a maximum of five 'implied characteristics' for each construct.

After completion of these measures, the subject pool was split into 9 groups of 6 subjects and 1 group of 8 subjects, as described below. No attempt could be made to balance groups for sex, except that if a group contained members of both sexes, it contained at least 2 members of each sex. These groups were dispatched to separate rooms where subjects were jointly to consider their Reptests, compare the constructs elicited by each member and generally to discuss the elements in order to pass on information. The rationale of this instruction was explained as intended to give subjects an idea of what others thought, while in fact it also allowed for interaction between members of the group in an atmosphere of evaluation and assessment of other persons. This was intended also to divert subjects' expectations of what was to follow (i.e. a Reptest where members of the group were elements). The reason for this is as follows. A rationale for the group arrangements had been provided by a study of the so-called Risky-Shift Phenomenon in the laboratory class previously. In that study, subjects had been split into groups for discussion and their post-discussion decisions had been compared with the pre-discussion ones. Accordingly, for this experiment, subjects were split into the same groups. It was hoped that this association might appear to subjects to be transparent and 'obvious' so that it would conjoin the purpose of diverting suspicion from what was to follow, with the purpose of providing opportunities for interaction. Post-experimental discussions revealed this to have been successfully achieved.

The nature of the groups is thus some way between a 'task-oriented' and a completely 'social' group; for while subjects did have a task before them, it was one where inner processes and subjective constructions were disclosed and not one where decisions were required. Furthermore, the success in arousing and diverting subjects' suspicions by the apparent transparency of the 'deception' in group composition imported a measure of informal discussion to the proceedings as became clear during de-briefing and class discussion. The nature of the groups is thus not as specifically task-oriented as may appear, and it lies somewhere at the low end of a continuum of 'social groups'. Since the atmosphere in the groups tends therefore towards the 'normal', one would predict more 'normal' patterns of construing to be exhibited during the last part of this study. However, the distance of subjects from each other in friendship means that normality cannot be predicted to be completely achieved.

After about 20 minutes had been allowed for this group activity, subjects were reassembled and given a second form of the Reptest. In this test, the elements were the other 5 members of the group (or in the case of the large group, any other 5 members of the group), and, as in the first Reptest, each element occurred twice on a 10 × 10 Reptest. The instructions for the completion of this test were the same as those for the first test.

When this measure had been taken, the subjects were informed that the experiment had terminated and they were de-briefed.

ANALYSIS AND RESULTS

The study has produced data which derive from subjects' consideration of 2 sets of elements who fall into the general category of non-intimate acquaintances. In one case, these persons had never met but were public figures known by repute. In the other case, subjects had met and briefly interacted with the elements construed, but firm friendships had not been established between members of the group. Both situations therefore provide the basis for further comparison with the situation where intimate and personally well-known acquaintances have been construed. Such comparisons will provide further evidence on the nature of the differences which emerge when construing those who are less well known. Since the 2 sets of elements construed here are in the same general category but yet different from each other in kind, they offer the opportunity not only for individual comparison with the normal, but for comparison with each other.

To effect such comparisons, all constructs from all subjects were classified into one of the 4 categories described in previous chapters—psychological, role, interaction or other constructs. The percentage of the total number of constructs which was represented by those in each of these 4 categories was then computed for later use. Furthermore, to provide a baseline for comparison with the classifications derived in this study, the data from the first part of Experiment F, which had been similarly classified earlier, were also reduced to percentages for easy comparison. This involves the assumption that a comparison can usefully be made between the 2 sets of data derived during physically different studies, but the comparability of age, qualifications, general status and 'occupation' of the 2 sets of subjects supports the inference that the 2 populations can be regarded as similar. The resulting percentages are given in Table 9.1.

Table 9.1. Percentages of constructs assigned to the four categories

| Test elements | | Construct types | | |
Experiment G	Psychological	Role	Interaction	Other
First test (distant public figures)	38·06	50·00	5·32	6·61
Second test (associates in discussion)	54·84	28·23	12·42	4·52
Baseline	63·04	24·42	6·24	6·40

(Data from Experiment F, where well-known others were construed.)

The comparison of the raw data (not percentages) from a test where well-known others were construed, and raw data from a test where two sets of non-intimate acquaintances were construed, was now effected by means of the Chi-squared Test for Independent Samples (Siegel, 1956). This gave $\chi^2 = 134·3817$, $df = 6$, $p < 0·001$, and indicates that, overall, there is a very pronounced difference between the 3 sets of scores. When this effect is partitioned off and the raw results from the previous experiment are tested against the raw results of the first Reptest here, the same test gives $\chi^2 = 94·1533$, $df = 3$, $p < 0·001$. This latter effect is largely due to differences in role and psychological construing and the nature of this effect was investigated later in the analysis. For the moment, the results of Experiment F were likewise compared with the data from the second Reptest, where subjects had construed the members of their discussion group. A similar picture emerged, for the test gave $\chi^2 = 20·1363$, $df = 3$, $p < 0·001$. In this case, however, most of the effect appeared to have been contributed by differences in numbers of interaction constructs. These results show that in both cases investigated in this study, whether subjects construe those whom they know distantly from the media, or those met and interacted with in task-like situations, a different distribution of constructs is observable from that shown when subjects construe those who are personally well-known. This finding thus casts more light on the different process involved at 'lower levels' of acquaintance.

However, these processes, while different from normal patterns, are not unitary in nature, and an indication is given by the results of the next test that even at 'lower levels' there are qualitative differences in construct distribution. A scrutiny of the first and second distributions of construct types derived in this experiment showed $\chi^2 = 76\cdot404$, $df = 3$, $p < 0\cdot001$. This clearly indicates differentiation of processes as a function of directness of knowledge. Such a finding substantiates the claim that studies of attraction to strangers met only briefly (for example, Byrne, Ervin and Lamberth, 1970; Senn, 1971; Mann, 1971) and studies of attraction to (mythical) strangers who are known only 'by repute' (for example, Byrne and Griffit, 1969; Tesser, 1971; Stroebe, Insko, Thompson and Layton, 1971) are not studies of the same phenomenon. The distinction shown at this level (as opposed to that already noted in Chapter 4 between 'attraction to strangers' and 'established friendship') is one which could usefully be attached to such work. For it is clear from Table 9.1, p. 106, that the distribution of construct types in the second test, while different from the baseline for normality, is a closer approximation to it than are the data derived from construal of distant others. The prediction was (p. 102) that this would be the case.

Another major purpose of this study, however, was to discover the uses to which subjects put the constructs which they generated in the first situation (i.e. from construing 'distant' public figures). To disclose this information, an analysis was made of the first part of the study, which had comprised a Reptest and a set of generated implications. Since the constructs on the Reptest had already been categorized into the 4 categories previously, the question as to the predominant category was already answered. It is clear from Table 9.1 that in this situation subjects use far more role constructs than either is normal or are used in the second situation. The hypothesis from previous discussion is that such constructs can nevertheless be the basis of implications of a psychological sort, and this was investigated by breaking all implications down into parts which could then be treated as constructs' positive poles, and classified in the same ways. Three independent raters achieved an agreement, as measured by Kendall's coefficient of concordance, of $w = 0\cdot9380$, $P < 0\cdot001$ in this breakdown of implications. The previously described quadripartite classification system was then applied and further analysis was made of these derived constructs as above. Percentages were also derived as before and are given in Table 9.2. The results of the test on the raw data confirmed the impression created by scrutiny of the percentage table and gave $\chi^2 = 69\cdot2596$, $df = 3$, $p < 0\cdot001$. Inspection of Table 9.2 indicates the direction of the difference and it is clear that the constructs derived as implications have produced greater amounts of psychological constructs at the expense of role constructs. The prediction is thus confirmed and the finding indicates that a 'psychological' use of basic and mundane role information can be made at the early levels of interaction.

Table 9.2. Percentages of constructs assigned to each category in order to compare
Reptest One with the derived implications

Test elements Experiment G	Construct types Psychological	Role	Interaction	Other
First test (distant public figures)	38·06.	50·00	5·32	6·61
Implications derived from these constructs	57·60	27·23	7·78	7·38
Baseline	63·04	24·43	6·24	6·40

(Data derived from Experiment F, where well-known others were construed.)

DISCUSSION

This experiment has had two main outcomes and one incidental product. It has shown that individuals do not merely assimilate information in acquaintanceships but they make use of it. Secondly, it has indicated further differentiation of types of acquaintance and shown that the original distinction (Chapter 4) between attraction and friendship may have been too simplistic. Incidentally, it has offered some confirmation for the view that the processes of 'person perception' are not at all distant from the processes displayed in early acquaintance and are available to PCT methods.

It is clear that subjects are prepared to make psychological use of non-psychological information or constructs which are generated about distant figures. This supports the view taken earlier, that the constructs used at first carry implications for superordinate construing. This invites the conjecture that these superordinate constructs give individuals the guidelines to similarities which he may expect to observe later and they thus constitute a powerful filter of acquaintances. The superordinate constructs also carry extensive implications by means of subordinate constructs, which can be examined for fitness as the interaction develops. For it is clear that the effects demonstrated here are evidence of the organization of information and closely allied to stereotyping. The stages of acquaintance need not be seen solely in terms of a reliance on different kinds of information, for the later stages also represent the creation of opportunities for testing the deeper levels of construing which have been suggested by mundane information. The 'stereotypes' presumably spring to mind as a convenient shorthand character sketch in order to facilitate prediction of behaviour, but the fluidity of interaction processes and the dynamics of construing inevitably create opportunities for the test and modification or individuation of these stereotypes.

But it is also clear that this formation of implications and cognitive leaps is a necessary part of the process, rather than an incidental one. For in the previous chapter it was shown that individuals largely eschewed psychological descriptives for new acquaintances and relied on the kind of mundane information which this study shows to be rich in psychological implications. This may functionalize the requirement to give acts a context. If someone acts ambitiously, the interpretation for the 'psychology' of it may depend on whether he wears a suit or an overall!

A further outcome of the study indicates further specialization in the types of interaction which can be studied, and it points to different kinds of construing in different kinds of situation. The situational relationship between construer and construed is evidently a strong influence on the constructs elicited and even within the class of situations which deal with subjects' reactions to strangers, there is room for differentiation. The nature of an intervening task seems to create changes in the character of a group and to invoke different patterns of construing behaviour. This point merits further investigation especially as the present studies suggest that a specific intervening task obstructs a subject's opportunities to test the hypotheses he has formed. A group orientation less related to a task seems indicated in order to remove some of the obstructions, in further studies. Even so, this possibility suggests one way in which potential friendships can be truncated. The contention in Chapter 3 was that all social interactions are potential friendship situations, and this latest discussion suggests some ways in which these potentialities can be curtailed. For we are not always given the *chance* to become close friends with the postman.

The observed patterns of construing thus represent the point reached in an evaluative strategy before the subjects' relevant construing processes were arrested by the end of the discussion. This suggests the hypothesis which can be investigated now: that had the group discussion started off as one more approximating to a 'true' social encounter, the processes which are tapped may have been developed in a way which more nearly resembles the 'normal' patterns previously discussed.

CONCLUSIONS

This discussion has some important implications for this 'area'. For it is clear that in measuring a subject's constructions of people whom he has just met, one runs the considerable risk of curtailing the free process of his evaluative capacities; and thus one stops short of the implicative structure with which such constructions are involved. This means that, because subjects' evaluative strategies have been given only restricted opportunity, have been used only briefly, and are quickly arrested in task-related situations, the measures which are employed can, at best, discover only the information on which subjects might base their evaluations and hypotheses. The measures will invariably stop short of being able to discover the evaluations and hypotheses themselves; and therefore they lose much that is of interest. (The situation has some affinities with a visit to the doctor which results in being told 'You have a rash' rather than 'You have measles'). The risk is clearly that the subordinate rather than superordinate descriptions are tapped and so the information disclosed may prove to be of lesser relevance in the understanding of subjects' likely behaviour than are the implications drawn by subjects from this information. Such implications and hypotheses would normally be tested later in the interaction, when more information had been gathered. Those reports in the literature where some allowance is made for some sort of interaction before attraction is measured would be regarded by this view as more reliable guides to the general processes of interpersonal attraction than those where no interaction is allowed. However, insofar as these arrest the development of the necessary types of construing, even these studies do not reflect normal processes. The success of the attitude studies alluded to earlier (Chapter 4) seems to depend, to an extent, on the fact that the method adopted (even when no interaction is permitted) misses out the early stages of filtering and concentrates on a later stage of the acquaintance process. The studies move straight into this stage by giving a subject the kind of information which he would have derived only after some time in a face-to-face interaction—the type of information argued here to be of most relevance to subjects in filtering their acquaintances at this stage. But even in face-to-face studies, the nature of an intervening task is clearly critical to group atmosphere.

One direction in which this points is to a testing of a typology of groups and its effect on friendship choices. The hypothesis is that a group allowed freely to discuss whatever it wishes, will represent a 'normal' situation more closely than others. This is predicted to allow usual filtering processes to operate more fruitfully. The opportunity for confirmation of derived implications may be conducive to their generation and operation. Such a situation would thus promote more useful and reliable filtering processes. This stance predicts that the search for similarity begins even at this point and that, in a group of this type, similarities should therefore be predictors of friendship choice.

10

An Examination of Early Filtering and Evaluation

In many of the situations examined so far in the testing of the hypothesis, the experiments have necessitated that subjects have before them a task involving discussion of some topic which has no subsequent relevance to the experiment. It has been included merely to provide the opportunity for interaction in a manner intended to involve all subjects as participants. However, the consequent interaction has been related to the task and no chance has yet been given for discussions of a more personal kind in a situation where there is no such topic for consideration.

To an extent, it could be claimed that important 'real-life' elements had been excluded from such tests which would restrict any general conclusions being drawn. Indeed, in a study of a special part of a process, one would expect this to be so. In this case, the 'real-life' aspect referred to would presumably be the more social kind of interaction which is observed in the Great Outside World. If this element of the G.O.W. were to be introduced to the laboratory, then subjects could conduct informal discussion in an atmosphere more redolent of the atmosphere which obtains during friendship formation. Naturally, it would be unscientifically generous to allow all subjects this freedom and only some will be permitted to enjoy it, so that its effects can be more rigorously pursued and studied. Similarly, since concern is still over the early information gathered, some limits will necessarily be imposed on the discussions, but in some cases these limits will be very insignificant.

The important point here is: what is this kind of information extracted and used *for*? The previous discussion would suggest that the creation of a stereotype is made possible thereby and this, in turn, creates a context within which individuation and correction can take place. However, another view is also possible. It may be the case that personal information may be important for its own sake and not for the use to which it is put. There is no direct way of ascertaining this from the previous experiments, and as a test of this possibility the present experiment concerns itself with two basic types of group: one where subjects were free to discuss any personal information they wished (these were called *Social Groups*); and the other where information of a personal kind was elicited from individual subjects in the presence of the other subjects in the group, who did not otherwise interact (these were called *Casual Groups*). Thus, in the one case, subjects could interact freely and unobserved and in the other they could not, but the instructions given to them all directed even the social groups to discuss the same type of information as that which was elicited in casual groups. Any differences would therefore be due to the effects of discussion and not merely the effects of information.

But the kind of topic given to the group for discussion may not be the only variable here, for in the real-life situation individuals have a reasonable expectancy of further interaction with those whom they have accepted as potential friends. Some experimental situations find this had to recreate and it has rarely been controlled, despite the work of Darley and Berscheid (1967), who found that expectancy of further interaction had an important effect on the subsequent attraction ratings. The present study therefore introduces a control for this factor and manipulates subjects' expectancies of interaction with the other subjects in their group. In order for this to be credibly accomplished, and for the reason that initial levels of interaction are to be studied, subjects were once again individuals who had no previous acquaintance with one another.

The expectancy of interaction clearly represents a dimension which makes the situation more akin to real-life friendship formation and gives the group a flavour which is absent from groups where members do not expect to interact again, and in this study the variables of group type (Social Groups and Casual Groups) and of expectancy (expectancy present or expectancy absent) provide the basis for a 2 × 2 design. The Social Group with expectancy present (Social-expectancy, for short) will be the group which most closely approximates to the real-life situation where discussion is unbounded and not task-related, and where the interaction is not limited to one encounter but carries the prospect of others. On the other hand, the Casual Group with expectancy absent (Casual-no-expectancy) most closely resembles situations with an unpromising basis for friendship. If we wish to arrange a typology of groups then the question must be answered whether a social atmosphere or the presence of expectancy is a more crucial ingredient in an interaction. On the present hypothesis the view must be that social atmosphere and free discussion matter more and therefore that the social groups hold a higher place in the hierarchy whose summit is this 'real-life'. The experimental groups can thus be seen in the hierarchy as follows, starting at the bottom with Casual-no-expectancy, Casual-expectancy, Social-no-expectancy and finally Social-expectancy. The Casual-no-expectancy and the Social-expectancy groups thus represent qualitatively different situations and it is the Social-expectancy group which is predicted to be the most realistic and reliable place for discovering the hypothesized relation between similarity and friendship choice. Several suggestions from previous chapters can now be put to the test.

METHOD FOR EXPERIMENT H

The investigation of situations where friendships have not yet developed, and where expectancies of interaction can be manipulated, requires the selection of subjects from as large population as possible in order to facilitate the exclusion of any established acquaintances. Study of previous friendship groups located in earlier experiments here revealed a size of about 6 or 7 to be about the norm and since the design necessitated 4 treatment groups, a number of subjects between 24 and 28 is indicated as most appropriate to represent real-life. It proved possible to select 27 subjects who were previously unacquainted with one another from a pool of volunteers attracted by advertisement. All subjects were undergraduate students aged between 18 and 23 years.

Subjects were split into 3 groups of 7 members and 1 group of 6 members and each group was dealt with on a separate occasion. Each group received only one combination of treatments in the 2×2 design where one variable was group type (Social or Casual) and the other was expectancy of interaction (present or absent). In Social Groups subjects were free to direct the discussion themselves in private; while Casual Groups were questioned publicly by the experimenter in order to give them the minimum opportunity for talking amongst themselves. Since subjects were unacquainted with one another before the experiment, credibility could be given to the statement (where applicable) that subjects would 'very likely never meet one another again' and expectancies could be manipulated as follows: in the 'expectancy' conditions, subjects were led to believe that they would partake in some group activity at a later stage of the experiment, using a (fictitious) test of the assessment of others. In the 'no expectancy' conditions, subjects were informed that they would complete further individual tests at a later stage of the experiment. Credibility was lent to these manipulations by overstating the length of time which subjects could expect to be spending in the experiment. The subjects nevertheless appeared relieved, rather than angry, when informed of the deceit in this respect.

INSTRUCTION OF SUBJECTS IN EXPERIMENT H

The instructions were the same for all subjects, except for the changes detailed below to effect the various manipulations.

Instructions in parentheses ( ) were given only to subject in the 'no expectancy' conditions; while those in strokes / / were given only to those in the 'expectancy' conditions. No subject had both sections 1 and 2 (below) read to them, but Social Groups heard section 1 and Casual Groups were read section 2. The full instructions were as follows:

'Thank you for coming this afternoon. As explained to you previously, the experiment will take between two and two-and-a-half hours, after which time you will be paid for participating. I shall now read you a set of printed instructions explaining what the experiment is about. Will you make sure that you understand the instructions fully, and to help you do this I will answer your questions at the end.

This is an experiment about how well people get to know things about one another in a limited space of time when . . .

> (They will very likely never meet one another again.)
> /they are going to need information about one another in order to perform an activity together later in the experiment, when cooperation will be important to success./

. . . There are three parts to the experiment, one of which will simply be the period when you can get some information about one another. You will have about half-an-hour to do this and then I shall give you three short tests which will enable me to see how successful you have been. The main part of the experiment will be explained in detail when we get to it, but essentially it is . . .

> (another set of forms to fill in, but this time with a very different rationale. These are intended to give a baseline level for some later work I am doing on person perception.)

> /a group activity, where you will be divided into successive pairs at random to compete with others on the Dimensions of Personal Judgement Test—the DPJ. This test involves making accurate assessments of other people./

. . . You will get further instructions later about these parts. But now the essence of the enterprise is for you to get to know things about one another. . .

> 1. I shall go away and leave you to it. While I am away, try to get to know things about one another as well as you can.

2. I shall ask you all some questions on biography, etc., in order to give you something to go on. Try to get to know things about one another as well as you can.

... You will find that the success of the later part of the experiment on...

(person perception)

/group performance on the DPJ test/

... will depend on it. Are there any questions?'

Subjects in the Social Groups were then left to discuss in private while subjects in the Casual Groups were asked in turn the same set of questions by the experimenter, in front of all other members of their group. These questions elicited the subject's name, university faculty, course of study and home town. Subjects were also asked what they thought of the town, how they liked the university life and how the town compared with home. They were encouraged to give expansive answers and to air their views.

When information transmission by one of these two methods had been allowed to take place for up to half-an-hour, subjects were given the 16×18 form of the Reptest, where the members of their group were elements, exactly as in Experiment F. When this had been completed, subjects were given an attraction choice test as follows. Subjects assigned each other member of their group a place on a 6-point scale as a measure of the likelihood of forming a friendship with each outside of the experimental situation. The scale ranged from 'most likely' (6) through 'likely' (5), 'not sure but possibly' (4), 'not sure, but possibly not' (3), 'unlikely' (2) to 'most unlikely' (1). Subjects were permitted to use each name once only and to place one name only in each of the six scalar categories, if possible. However, they were permitted to give a 'first choice' and 'other choices' for a category if they felt that it was more representative to put two (or more) other subjects into the same category and therefore leave (at least) one other category unfilled. These measures were introduced as tests of the subjects' success in assimilating information about the others and in all cases were treated as a minor concern in the experiment, with the 'big part' yet to come.

When these measures had been completed, subjects were expecting another hour or so of experimentation as 'the main part of the experiment'. Nevertheless, they were now told that the experiment had ended, were debriefed and paid for taking part. It was clear from the subjects' comments at this point that the manipulations had been successfully effected and subjects had really anticipated further experimental activity. Other remarks during debriefing revealed that the 'expectancy' manipulation had similarly succeeded and that some subjects even felt anxiety about their expected performance on the 'DPJ test'. The intention to equate types of information available in the two types of group was also empirically supported by enquiries as to the type of information discussed by the Social Groups.

ANALYSIS AND RESULTS

The type of friendship choice discussed here is clearly 'attraction to strangers', and it is plain that the sociometric data here do not in any sense represent firm friendships—indeed, the definition of mutual choice here would be very unclear. At this stage, therefore, it is acceptable to use the data from the attraction test only cautiously and in a way that is different from the norm in the previous experiments. Two uses are made of the data: in one case the numbers given to all the six scalar categories described above (1 : 'most unlikely to form a friendship' to 6 : 'most likely to form a friendship') were used to assess attraction level (see below); in the other case, choices in only the positive categories (from 6: 'most likely' to 4 : 'not sure, but possibly') were counted as instances of attraction, and similarity to the attractive others was assessed as described below.

One main part of the analysis required consideration of the distribution of constructs, not only to discover differences in the experimental groups as functions of expectancy and group type but also to allow a comparison of some of the data from this experiment with some from a previous one, where appropriate. The analysis thus departs again from the norm of these experiments and concentrates here on construct types (as assigned to the categories described in earlier chapters: psychological, role, interaction, other). Only later does the analysis revert to the usual overall method. Accordingly, at this stage all constructs were classified into the quadripartite typology used previously (Chapter 9).

The experiment presents three main directions for analysis: first, a comparison of data from groups where subjects had no expectancy of further interaction (including data from a previous experiment); second, an investigation of the effects of group type and expectancy on the predominant categories of construing; and third, a study of the effects of these two latter factors on similarity and friendship. In the first analysis, the comparison of three group types was effected by study of the two groups in the 'no expectancy' condition in this experiment and a group from Experiment F, where subjects discussed Choice Dilemma problems. The findings of Experiments F and G can thereby be amplified and supplementary evidence may be gathered on the nature of progressive change in construct types. The groups considered can be arranged logically as follows: Casual (where no interaction occurred, as in the present experiment); then Interaction (where task-related interaction occurred as in discussion of the Choice Dilemma problems in Experiment F); then Social (where 'free' discussion and interaction were permitted). These groups then represent a progression from a simple, very basic, information-related situation to a less restricted situation which represents a real-life situation in terms of the literature. Accordingly, in order to provide a group for comparison from Experiment F, one group of 7 subjects was picked at random and their data used in the comparison test. The raw data were submitted to a χ^2 test for K independent samples, which gave the very highly significant result of $\chi^2 = 136 \cdot 2448$, $df = 6$, $p < 0 \cdot 001$, which is further evidence that group type affects the type of constructs which individuals use to describe fellow members of their group. 'Attraction to strangers' can now be suggested to cover several subtly different phenomena, whose distinction is sometimes obscured by the use of a single class name.

The above raw data were converted to percentages 'for easy viewing' and tabulated. The percentages of the total constructs used by each group, which resulted from each particular type of construct, are given in Table 10.1, which also gives a baseline set of percentages. These latter were derived from the construing of well-known acquaintances performed by the present comparison group from Experiment F.

Table 10.1. Percentages of construct types used by the three groups with no expectancy of further interaction

| Groups | Construct types | | | |
	Psychological	Role	Interaction	Other
Social	24·79	57·02	8·26	9·91
Interaction*	20·37	24·14	50·00	6·49
Casual	9·00	88·28	0·92	1·80
Baseline*	65·81	29·06	1·71	3·42

* The baseline data and the data from the interaction group are derived from Experiment F. For this present comparison, one group from Experiment F was picked at random—see text.

The second part of the analysis investigated the major effects of group type and expectancy levels on the responses of all the subjects in the present experiment only. Each type of constructs was taken separately and submitted to a two-way analysis of variance which examined Expectancy × Group Type. The amounts of *psychological construing* were significantly affected by Group Type ($F = 6 \cdot 620585$; $df = 1$, 24; $p < 0 \cdot 025$) but not by Expectancy Level. *Role constructs* were sensitive to the interaction of Group Type and Expectancy. Thus, the number of role constructs decreased significantly between the Casual Group with 'no expectancy' and the one where 'expectancy' was present ($F = 12\cdot3415$; $df = 1$, 24; $p < 0\cdot01$). Within the 'no expectancy' condition, the Social Group used significantly fewer role constructs than did the Casual Group ($F = 7\cdot935$; $df = 1$, 24; $p < 0\cdot01$). There were no significant effects of either treatment on *Interaction constructs* or on *Other constructs*.

Table 10.2. Percentages of construct types used by the four groups in Experiment H

| Groups | Construct types | | | |
	Psychological	Role	Interaction	Other
Casual				
No expectancy	9·00	88·28	0·90	1·80
Expectancy	13·02	76·71	7·27	2·89
Social				
No expectancy	24·79	57·02	8·26	9·91
Expectancy	24·80	61·60	8·80	4·80
Baseline*	65·81	29·06	1·71	3·42

* The baseline data are derived from the randomly chosen group from Experiment F and represent the percentages of construct types generated in construing well-known others.

Such results as these invite one to look more closely at the data; and from such an inspection the following picture emerges (see Table 10.2). Within a given level of Expectancy, the differences between group types appear to be in terms of the number of psychological and role constructs used. In Social Groups, nearly 25 per cent of constructs are psychological and about 60 per cent are role, whereas the percentages are roughly 10 per cent and 82 per cent, respectively, in the Casual Groups. With respect to Social Groups only, it appears that the difference between 'no expectancy' and 'expectancy' lies in variation which increases the number of Role constructs at the expense of Other constructs, although in absolute terms the effect is paltry (and non-significant). In the case of Casual Groups, however, this same change in expectancy results in an increase of psychological and interaction constructs at the expense of the previously 'oversubscribed' category of Role constructs. This results in a closer approximation to the figures recorded for the Social Groups and is empirical evidence which operationalizes the intuitively arranged 'hierarchy' of groups proposed in the introduction to this study. Thus it appears that the manipulated difference in expectancies was successful in giving the Casual-Expectancy Group a character which was moved from the baseline some little way towards a more social type; so, correspondingly, have the proportions of constructs been observed to shift some little way towards a pattern more similar to (although still some distance from) that in Social Groups. But even the Social Groups in this experiment show patterns a long way short of those in the natural situation (as represented by the baseline derived from the group randomly selected from Experiment F).

This evidence indicates further ways in which group orientation is responsible for differences in reported construing, and when taken together with that already presented (Chapters 8 and 9) begins to make the way clearer for a definite hypothesis on the nature of changes in processes during acquaintanceship. For it is even more detrimental to the view that the tapping of 'early' processes can tell us anything of direct value about later ones, in the sense that it further emphasizes the need for clarity on the relationship betweeen studies of attraction to strangers and those of the later stages of friendship.

In an attempt not only to measure the stages of acquaintance in more detail, but also to gauge their effect on the amounts of similarity observed and the concomitant effects on friendship choices, further analysis was concerned directly with the actual content, rather than with the type, of constructs used. For this third stage of the analysis those constructs of every member of a given group which were remaining after the eliminations described earlier (p. 61) were compared with those of each other member of their group. Similarities of the construct content (see Chapter 6, p. 61) were measured for all constructs, and no separate analysis was made here for constructs of the psychological type. When scores for each possible pairing had been accounted for, an analysis was initiated to discover the effects of the 2×2 treatments on the scores obtained. A two-way analysis of variance revealed the following significant effects. Expectancy Level was found to have a significant effect on the number of similarities observed ($F = 6.074839$; $df = 1$, 24; $p < 0.025$), with the lower numbers of observed similarities occurring in the 'expectancy' condition. A very highly significant effect of Group Type was found ($F = 164.4192$; $df = 1$, 24; $p < 0.001$), with Social Groups demonstrating fewer similarities than Casual Groups. In addition, a significant interaction effect was observed ($F = 31.18761$; $df = 1$, 24; $p < 0.01$) and when this was partitioned off, it became clear that variance was mainly contributed by differences attributable to the effects of Group Type, within the 'no expectancy' condition ($F = 169.4123$; $df = 1$, 24; $p < 0.001$). In both Expectancy conditions the Casual Group manifested more intermember similarities than in the Social Group. The finding will be discussed later as due in large measure to the types of construct used in the two groups. However, the effects of differences in expectancy are different in the two types of group, which points again to the need for clarity about the type of group and the type of similarity under scrutiny in such research. Casual Groups showed a decrease in similarities as function of the increase in expectancy level

($F = 32 \cdot 39568$; $df = 1$, 24; $p < 0 \cdot 01$), while similarity between members of the Social Groups increased ($F = 4 \cdot 866772$; $df = 1$, 24; $p < 0 \cdot 05$).

Tests to discover the effects of level-of-friendship choice were next undertaken, and for this purpose a three-way analysis of variance was conducted (Group Type × Expectancy × Level-of-Friendship as factors affecting Similarity scores). All tests gave non-significant results and indicated that at this stage different levels of friendship choice were not mediated by the different levels of similarity between subjects. The meaning of this finding is unclear at this stage and will be discussed below in relation to some further analysis.

DISCUSSION OF EXPERIMENT H

The above results show that it is not merely depth of knowledge which can account for the obtained differences but that some influence of 'group intent' or 'group atmosphere' can be discerned. In other words, the type of information, the way it is transmitted and the type of things which the group members do as a group have now all been shown to be influences on the assessment processes which individuals apply to their confederates. Similarly, the processes in the new and developing interaction can be seen to represent those which occur in the new and developing friendship. Initially the information used is pedestrian: height, hair colour, dress, nationality, for example, and it is presumably the case that individuals have different biases as to the quality and quantity of information which they gather at this stage. Such observations are not without their implications for higher-level construing (as argued in the previous chapter) and this view accords with such comments as 'People's dress gives you a lot of information about their character', or 'I can sum up a person just by looking at his face' which are well-known chestnuts of popular 'psychologizing'. Whatever information is surveyed at this stage, the hypothesis is that at a higher level and later stage of processing, an individual begins to take note of the interaction style of a new acquaintance. Does he speak loudly or softly? Is there an accent? Does he wave his arms? The above results suggest that as individuals become more involved in a situation which resembles real-life acquainting, such information as they have accrued leads them on to higher-level construing and inference. Psychological constructs are typically those where assessment and evaluation are made and where some generalizations and inferences are drawn (for example, constructs having as one pole 'shallow', 'settled and sensible', 'thoughtful', 'a stable character'). The present study finds that this type of construct is used more by the Social Groups, where 'real life' interaction was permitted. In this case, the accrued information has been synthesized and coordinated and the questions have by then become: 'Is he shy?', 'Does he have a Northerner's outlook?', 'Is he excitable or merely demonstrative?'

The fuller exposition of the import of this hypothesis will be reserved for a subsequent chapter, but even at this stage it must be pointed out that it is not even implicit in this view that any one type of process need be confined to, or discrete from any one stage. A predominance of certain types of activity has been recorded above at certain stages, but several types of use can be made of the same type of information, as was argued in the introductory chapters and realized in Chapter 9, p. 107: but it has so far been the aim of this study to investigate the types of information used. The further question of how these proposed stages reflect in a microcosmic way the things which occur in a developing acquaintance will also be considered in relation to the previous discussion (Chapter 7) of the possibility that developing friendships are themselves microcosmic representations of the way in which construing processes develop ontogenetically.

The results discussed above are specific and useful support for the contention made earlier that the generality of findings on 'friendship' is, at best, limited as a function of the recognition that there are different stages of friendship with different processes involved. Thus, insofar as the situation mirrors real life, it has been shown possible to use PCT methods to uphold the 'filtering' view and disclose stages of acquaintance where different filters apply. The question now is whether these different filters are sufficient causes of friendship in a way which is *not* predicted by the hypothesis, in other words whether they are independent of similarity, or whether (in spite of or after them) it is similarity which is ultimately important. The findings above on the stages of acquaintance are, therefore, only one of the outcomes of this experiment, which was also concerned to study the nature of, and changes in, construct similarity as a function of Group Type and Expectancy. In order to discover this a fairly complex argument must be unfolded in order to show the relative statures of the Groups (in terms of G.O.W. simulation and 'reality') and the effect which this has on the similarities observed.

From the second part of the analysis it is apparent that the effect of increasing expectancy level in Social Groups is to concentrate the subjects' attention on those constructs which facilitate inference (since Social Groups abandon unclear constructs—in the Other category—in favour of more informational constructs—in the Role category—while still maintaining Psychological construing at a fairly constant level—see Table 10.2). In the case of Casual Groups, the subjects' attention is altered by higher expectancy more towards constructs which are themselves inferential (i.e. the Psychological constructs) in an attempt to achieve a more 'normal' distribution of construct types. Where there is change it is in the direction of convergence of the two groups; but this means nothing in the absence of a baseline. From the table of percentages for this experiment (Table 10.2, p. 118), it can be seen that while the two groups seem to be converging to similar levels and percentages of construct types, these levels are nevertheless very far from the normal ones. Those percentages derived previously in Chapter 9 from a baseline 'normal situation' group are also included for easy comparison. Thus it is apparent just how far a reduced situation can reflect different processes from the ones used when describing elements who are well known. The results of Experiment F have shown that the type of constructs used of new acquaintances does not adequately reflect the totality of possibilities open to the subject at a later stage of friendship and Experiment G has shown that this is a function of the elements described and the processes involved rather than anything artefactually produced. Rather, in a situation such as this, it appears that the aim of each individual (if the present hypothesis holds water) is to discover the extent of the similarities which exist between himself and another person, in order to see how firmly based a friendship would be possible between them. One would thus expect that in this experiment as expectancy level increases, so the search for significant similarities would increase, and individuals' speculations about friendship outcomes would operate in parallel. The results (p. 119) do indicate that this expectation is well-founded, but it occurs only in the Social Groups, as the third stage of the analysis reveals. Casual Groups actually show a decrease in similarity scores as expectancy level increases, but one could argue that this is tied to the decrease in role construing (and thus to decrease in similarity of 'factual' information) which has tended to inflate similarity scores in the Casual-no expectancy conditions, where Role construing is high. In such Casual Groups, subjects use mainly 'information-related' constructs as has been pointed out above and this will tend to create overlap, for the reason that the design lays the same information of this sort at the subjects' disposal. Although able simultaneously to 'interpret' such information (and thereby to give their constructs more of an individual flavour which would differentiate their Reptest from the bog of similarities of factual information) they do not do so in the way that Social Groups have been shown to do. This was argued to be due to a lack of opportunity for the test of such interpretation (see previous chapter), and any desire to eschew cautious inspection and test does not seem to be a very powerfully operationalized one. Thus, as the crux of the complex argument, now unfolded, one can suggest that the type of similarity in the two types of group is of a different sort from one another. That in the Social Group is, perhaps, a more important sort.

If the above crucial argument is true, then it should be possible to find an effect of the increase in similarity in the Social Groups as follows. It has been a cornerstone of the argument here that increases in construct similarity in a situation, such as Social-expectancy, which more nearly reflects the situation in real life, must be taken to create increased attraction. Thus the hypothesis predicts here that individuals in the Social-expectancy Group who are more similar to another subject in terms of construct content, will choose that subject and be chosen by him. For the purpose of testing this prediction, friendship choices on the sociometric test were reduced to one of two sets. Those choices with a positive loading on the test (i.e. those in categories 6, 5 and 4) were counted as attraction choices while those with a negative attraction loading were scored as rejections. This provided the rationale on which subjects could be counted as friendship pairs or nominal pairs as before, and allowed the basic methods used previously, to be applied here too. However, it is clear that the criteria for 'friendship' are very far removed from those adopted so far and the method of operationalizing attraction is rather more similar to that reflected in many of Byrne's experiments, reported in Byrne (1969).

A direct test of the prediction is now possible and so the mean number of similarities scored in friendship pairs was compared with the number derived from nominal pairs, within the Social-expectancy Group. As previously, the two sets of scores were submitted to a t-test and in this case it was found that $t=2.902$, $df=6$, $p<0.05$. The prediction has thus been confirmed in its claim that similarities of construing would differentiate friendship and nominal pairs in a group of this type. However, to test the possibility that other groups in this experiment had manifested this effect (which is *not* predicted by the hypothesis), the scores of all other groups were similarly treated. As can be seen from Table 10.3, the Social Expectancy Group was the only one which showed a significant difference on this test. This result shows that the filters so far identified by the differences in construing are not *ipso facto* different sufficient causes of attrac-

Table 10.3. A test of the differences between the number of similarity scores derived from friendship and nominal pairs within a given group

| Condition of expectancy | Group type | |
	Casual	Social
No expectancy	$\overline{X}_D = -0.7842$	$\overline{X}_D = 0.0983$
	$SD\overline{X}_D = 1.2265$	$SD\overline{X}_D = 0.7545$
	$t = -1.6919$ NS	$t = 0.3191$ NS
Expectancy	$\overline{X}_D = -0.3783$	$\overline{X}_D = 1.0728$
	$SD\overline{X}_D = 1.9753$	$SD\overline{X}_D = 0.9783$
	$t = -0.4691$ NS	$t = 2.9018*$

* $p < 0.05$, $df = 6$.

tion at this level, but that the further premise of the filtering-similarity hypothesis is required. The results thus support the similarity hypothesis, just as the previously discussed analysis supports the filtering hypothesis.

CONCLUSIONS

This study has sustained the disclosure of underlying processes in situations designed to approximate to early acquaintance in a way which other measures (e.g. measurement of attitudes) might tend to obscure. The view that similarity is a reinforcer on its own, undeniable, unassailable and automatic, denies us the chance to bring out many nuances and differences incorporated in subjects' perceptions of differences in groups and situations. By treating such situations as laboratory replicas of real life (even scale models) with 'given' values, rather than situations which subjects must, as usual, interpret for themselves, one runs the risk of hiding the importance of a situation's effects on subjects' percepts and processes in a way which a measure of their construing can bring to light. By this means, evidence has now been gathered to illuminate the way in which an interaction or acquaintance progresses. It has been shown that concentration on 'factual information' tends to shift towards a certain amount of interest in interaction style, which in turn makes way for a greater predominance of psychological and higher-order construing. The course of studies has also produced results to suggest that these findings are not artefacts of the restricted situations but fit into a wider picture. From them it is clear that the evidence which is gathered at early stages is used to produce inferences which make it easier to progress to a higher level of construing which eschews factual information in preference for more 'psychological' description.

This evidence sprang from, and can now be referred to, the previous findings (Chapter 7) on differences observed at the different times in the developing friendships studied earlier in depth. The finding there was that at early stages of friendship after some preliminary real life interactions, some overall similarity of constructs could be observed between pairs of subjects who later became friends. This finding has been replicated here in a much reduced situation and this succeeds in demonstrating just how early in acquaintance such processes occur. Further, it shows that as topics of study in their own right, such reduced situations can be made to *reflect* the occurrences of the G.O.W. somewhat and to show something of the nature of the information, evidence and processes utilized at the very early and basic stages of acquaintanceship.

11

The Filtering Theory Reconsidered and Developed

SOME INTRODUCTORY CAVEATS

In view of the espousal of Kelly's dynamic outlook at an earlier point, it is hardly surprising that during the experimental reports certain aspects of the original position have been transformed, amended, corrected, supplemented, developed or quietly suppressed. Indeed, it is encouraging. For it is clear that while some detailed points have required reassessment, the basic position has been supported in many of its suggestions. Yet before launching hopefully into a discussion of the relevance of this approach to the G.O.W. in ways which may not already be obvious, efficiency demands the tightening of some of the logical joints of the theory; the investigation of some of its limitations and advantages; and the assessment of ways in which it may be developed. In a phrase, its internal utility must be re-examined in the light of the accumulated evidence.

It is, of course, for the reader to apply his own particular judgements on the value of the theory. In the first instance, however, the theory's standpoint and attendant limitations might properly be judged against the kind of criteria which were originally set for the theory to match. Theoretically, these criteria devolved around integration: that is to say, an original intention was to produce and substantiate a theory wherein explanations of man's general behaviour might be integrated with explanations of his activity in friendship formation. It was also hoped to integrate these explanations with those which may be offered in other areas of psychology and to incorporate the whole within a personality theory. Such criteria have been suggested for any theory of friendship formation, and are not limited to apply here only (Duck, 1972 (b)), for the issues are such that theoretical rather than empirical resolution of them can be achieved initially. On a related practical level, criteria were essentially concerned with relevance to real life. An extension of the above argument was that the same kind of explanation need be offered for normal behaviour and behaviour in the laboratory. This is a separate point from the specious claim that laboratory experiments do not reflect real life ('putting tokens in experimental boxes does not reflect Altruism') and it is framed at a different level. For there is a sense in which laboratory and normal processes are examples of one another, as argued in Chapters 1 and 2. Some caution must therefore be exercised in the handling of arguments on artificiality, since the obvious claim runs the risk of over-simplifying the issues and, for example, assuming that life and lab are discrete areas of 'real life' unless consciously and diligently related to one another.

It is such complexities which have unfolded in the course of the present series of studies, and the problem now appears to be very similar to that which confronted social man in Chapter 1: how to deal with a mass of complications in a convenient manner. The present answer is the same as his: namely, to simplify and condense things by the use of general labels. Despite such simplifications which are perforce required, it is appropriate here to repeat the warnings issued earlier that talk of 'stages' in acquaintance should not be allowed to mislead one into imagining that the stages are seen to be discrete, separate, clearly ordered or anything of that kind. The present approach still holds to the view that minor and major fluxes in emphasis are continually occurring within and during acquaintance, but that some emphases gradually recede in value for the agent as their advantages for hypothesis and their contributions to explanation of observed behaviour become less obvious. Indeed, the evidence of the present studies is that such changes occur at extremely subtle levels (cf. Chapters 7 et seq.). This specification allows us to assert that the same stage may not be reached by both participants to an interaction at the same time. It will be argued below (Chapter 12) that some 'acquainters' are more equal than others and the particular way in which 'social experts' are conceived will be given closer attention. However, pending further empirical evidence, it is taken to be generally true that these emphatic fluxes occur in all acquaintances and that some types of construing fade more rapidly than others. Particularly, this will be true of early constructs such as physicalistic ones, on which whole structures of hypothesis may be erected in the early parts of interaction for later test. The experiments here show that this kind of cue loses its force as the interactors become more concerned over psychological attributes and attribution. However, too simple a view of the 'stages' suggestion may obstruct the possibility of accounting for the fact that, for example, changes in physical characteristics have profound or superficial effects on a person's behaviour (disfigurement, boils, etc.) and may require to be brought into the constructive framework of even an established friend, who would normally have passed by the reliance on physical assessment. It is also clear that one may, after a while, become aware of a physical attribute which an acquaintance perceives as affecting his dealings with others (as when a close friend may confess a previously unsuspected physical condition, such as arthritic pain, or persistent headaches, which may be seen by him to afflict his social behaviour). Realization of its existence may influence subsequent or retrospective 'psychological' construing of his activities or 'motivations'.

When reassessing the earlier claims of the theory it may also be important to reiterate the distinction drawn between necessary and sufficient conditions for friendship formation. Some approaches (see Chapter 1) might seem to suggest (sometimes explicitly, sometimes implicitly) that if a given situation or factor obtains then friendship formation will *inevitably* begin. Earlier it was claimed that this allows too little respect for an individual's rationality and it is wiser to invest individuals with the powers to hypothesize and interpret and to concede that these may influence or define their behaviour. In terms of 'filters', this means that individuals may weigh up cues which seem important to them and they may then act in the light of these deliberations. Indeed, an extension of the Festingerian position adopted in Chapter 1 would be to claim that one aspect of early filtering may be 'relevance-orientation'. In other words, that they may operate to weed out those persons with whom a later cognitive and constructive comparison would be felt undesirable, inappropriate or strictly risible. If so, a prediction might follow that *at an early stage*, putative acquaintances may choose others who appear similar to their 'ideal self' but later may prefer to found their evaluations and comparisons on perceived similarities between 'real self' and other. While there is as yet no direct evidence which bears on this point from the present hypothesis, some tangential evidence is provided by Beier, Rossi and Garfield (1961) who found that subjects projected more socially desirable and ideal characteristics on to friends. However, at just the conceptual level, this point enlarges an additional complexity to the simple distinction between necessary and sufficient conditions for friendship.

An additional intricacy also confronts the development of any theory of friendship formation in the light of evidence from Chapters 6, 7 and 8 on the differences and similarities between friendship formation in the two sexes, not only as a function of sex but also as a function of the kind of person with whom the acquaintance is developed. The findings here were that, while males and females appear to gather the same kinds of information at the early stages and to use the same overall strategies (i.e. filtering and similarity) when forming friendships with members of the same sex, when it comes to cross-sex pairings females adopt these above methods but males do not (or do not *yet*, for females may be quicker to construe males in terms of psychological constructs than are males when construing females). While this finding must not be divorced from the remembrance of the age of the subjects involved (about 20 years), it is nevertheless an interesting finding that such effects occur at all and it compels recognition of the labyrinthine nature of this area of study.

A frequently recurrent theme here has been the relation between areas of psychology which for various reasons not all perverse or purblind (for example, reduction for convenience) have been regarded as separate. The involution of this approach is to indicate the many levels at which these areas contribute to the processes of friendship formation. For example, the perception of others with the intention of evaluating them as potential friends involves processes which have been separated for analysis in the area of person perception. This necessary simplification of phenomena for study must not mislead us into taking it separately perforce at the theoretical level. Nor is one arguing that these two areas need to be recombined. They always have been combined in the phenomena of friendship formation, but it is necessary to *recognize* that they have been so. Similarly, because the processes of friendship formation involve language, thought, implicit personality theories, etc., these must be allowed at least to permeate our explanations of friendship formation. Each may impinge at a different level or stage and may be of relevance at specific points (e.g. only in 'attraction'), in specific conditions (e.g. when interaction continues), for specific people (e.g. adults), etc., but space must be left in our explanations for such things to intrude. The present view's espousal of PCT may enlarge the possibilities for these kinds of integration, since work on these kinds of topic has already been completed from a PCT viewpoint. The adoption of our armchair view of social behaviour in Chapter 1 has paved the way for a consideration of some of the other levels with which theories of friendship formation must be concerned. For friendship formation can never be seen as taking place in a vacuum. Just as a complete understanding of phonetics can never be achieved by studying language in total isolation from the suppositions and assumptions which must pervade the *use* of language in a social setting (Rommetveit, 1972), so it makes little sense to attempt, for whatever purpose, to isolate friendship formation as a phenomenon from its social setting and the kinds of explanation which can be given of social behaviour. At the present stage of sophistication this theoretical complexity may have to be paid empirical lip-service, but even this is slightly better than ignoring it altogether. In this way a theory can hope to explain not only *why* but *how* people become friends.

In the light of such considerations one becomes aware of how simplified an approach is represented in the reduction of such complexities for study. However, to an extent, some of the deleterious effects of this necessity can be attenuated by theoretical attempts to retain the complication. In other words, one may, to an extent only, alleviate the effects of reduction by retaining theoretical complexity and by adopting a theory of personality and social behaviour which incorporates and explains simultaneously laboratory behaviour and normal processes.

We are now faced with a paradox. At one and the same time it is necessary to simplify and to complicate our outlook. For in order to suppress the mushrooming imbroglio of the topic, one has espoused reduction of the topic to 'convenience' headings. But awareness of this process may simultaneously heighten awareness of the topic's complexities. The above caveats are therefore given not only because (at one level) they serve to specify some points of difficulty in the theory (e.g. it is too vague: are all friendships based on the same mechanisms?), but also because (at another level) they warn us about what is involved in the reassessment of these difficulties (i.e. an increase in complexity). As previously, they may be tackled logically by starting with the general problems which would affect any theory and then working towards the particular problems of methodology which require to be dealt with. Such general problems concern the paradigm for study; the use of 'determinant factors' in explanation; interpretation of phenomena; and artificiality. Specific problems of methodology can then be seen more clearly against a background.

GENERAL PROBLEMS IN A THEORETICAL DEVELOPMENT

The lack of consensus on the paradigm case of 'interaction' for study in this context originally suggested the view that there could be no satisfactory single paradigm and that to try to 'produce' one was to obscure too many of the important variables. The literature was claimed to be starting to take the view similar to that expressed by Byrne, Ervin and Lamberth (1970, p. 158): 'Whether the determinants of first impressions are precisely the same as the determinants of prolonged friendship, of love or of marital happiness is an empirical question, and one requiring a great deal of research.' The original bisection of phenomena into early acquaintance and long friendships of distinctive types is supported by the evidence presented in Chapter 6 where the results suggested the simple view and showed that at the early stages of developing friendships, similarity was observed between types of constructs which were later superseded by others. However, the later studies indicated a greater diversity of processes and that it was not *just* a concentration on different types of similarity which functionalized the distinction between 'acquaintance' and 'developed friendship'. Experiment F (Chapter 8) showed the existence of a different emphasis at very early stages and similarity was not then of so much importance as was a concentration on interaction styles. This finding was supported by Experiment H where the evidence indicated several changes in the emphases of construing as a function of group-type and expectancy. Only the most 'real' of all the groups investigated under controlled circumstances showed any embryonic relation between similarity and friendship choices. These results, taken together, thus indicate a greater complexity of variables than has been discussed in the literature, and while the above bald dichotomy, between short-term and long-term acquainting is not refuted by such results, its phrasing appears to obscure this multiformity of types and levels and degrees of shorter and longer 'friendships'. The further implications of this view remain for investigation, but the adoption of the more 'sophisticated' view has been assisted by the findings of the above studies which compound the paradox by clarifying in general and yet leading to awareness of our ignorance of detail.

This kind of obscurity is further increased by the implicit view that a consistent and single-minded approach is taken by individuals throughout encounters, whether a search for similarity (Byrne, 1969), or for complementarity (Winch, 1958; Rychlak, 1965), or for positive evaluation (Walster and Walster, 1963), or for comparable levels of self-esteem (Jacobs, Berscheid and Walster, 1971). It has become clear during the course of these studies that just as the terms 'attraction' and 'friendship' cover a variety of situations, so too does the usual search for consistently employed 'factors' obscure the variability which influences individuals during acquaintance, and has overshadowed the importance of accounting for the subjective weighting of these factors. While such things as interaction-frequency may be of importance in continuing acquaintance, the view that no such 'factor' is sufficient on its own to produce friendship (the second basic assumption of the present view) has also received support. In Chapter 10 it was reported that differences in the types of interaction experienced by individuals had marked influences on the outcomes for them. The effects of expectancy and the type of group in which a subject found himself, lend credence to the view that there are significant shifts of emphasis both in the strategies of individuals at different stages and also in their focus of concern. Some form of subjective evaluation of 'factors' and some subjective structuring of them in terms of personal importance seems to be a necessary concomitant of the filtering hypothesis. For while it is clear that there are different 'stages' in the acquaintance process, it is equally clear that there are also functional changes in emphasis, with subjects appearing to look for different information and to make use of it to create a whole picture. In terms of the theory, they make use of these 'factors' to filter the individuals whom they encounter.

The third assumption of the theory is clearly the most central and is aligned directly with the basic position of Kelly's (1955) theory. This is the view that all phenomena—as the etymology of the word suggests—take their meaning from 'how they *appear* to the individual'. The domain of man's rationality is thus extended to his interpretation of even the minutiae of his world, and his world (even in the laboratory) is personally represented to him in terms of and by his constructs of it (see Chapters 1 and 2). The reason why no 'factor' is solely sufficient for friendship is simply this: that each piece of information, etc., must be interpreted and evaluated by each individual and in terms of its context or the 'stage' reached. Each may at any time be given any weight—even a different weight from that normally associated with it. As a simple example, individuals may choose to overlook some negatively evaluated interaction technique, such as stammering or shyness, in view of their expectation of eventual positive outcomes from the 'cognitive similarity' which they suspect to lie beneath this awkward surface apparently presented to them. Even Churchill had a speech impediment! It therefore seems necessary to allow for subjects' evaluation processes in experimental studies where this aspect of perception is not deliberately to be controlled for. In this light it seems a dangerous policy not to allow subjects to generate free responses, since this may invite the possibility of overlooking basic features of any acquaintance-process. Comparisons of free-response (Reptest) methods and those where subjects merely answer pre-set questions, have been made in Chapter 6 and offer support for this view. Such findings are compounded by implication in the other studies, however, since many of the later findings could be derived from 'provided question' tests only with extreme difficulty and contortion (for example, the findings that individuals consciously restrict their normal construing processes when dealing with new acquaintances).

Furthermore, those methods which rely on measuring subjects' interpretations of phenomena can rebut the charge of artificiality somewhat more effectively than can other methods. For the PCT approach is laboratory-oriented only insofar as it requires subjects to verbalize those processes which PCT takes to be natural and indeed natural continuations of the processes used in everyday activity. Those methods which require intensive self-examination or the imaginary placement of oneself into contingent yet generalizable events (e.g. 'I would be willing to describe myself as a pretty "strong" personality'; 'I have never seen a vision'; 'I would never play cards (poker) with a stranger'; 'If given the chance I would make a good leader of people'; 'I am not afraid of picking up a disease or germs from doorknobs') may be heightening a subject's awareness of the essentially peculiar nature of his task. On a related issue, subjects in the present studies did not normally have their attraction levels manipulated (cf. Chapter 3) and merely recorded their version of the facts. A further possible artificiality is thus attenuated. An example may illuminate these points more brightly. In Experiment C subjects were required to indicate their awareness of any similarity between their own construct system and their acquaintances' (Chapter 6, p. 69); but in the Byrne and Griffit

(1969) study, subjects were required to fill up a Repression-Sensitization Scale as a perfect (indeed, mythical) stranger may have done, given that either 20 per cent or 50 per cent or 80 per cent of his responses were reported to have been similar to the subject's. The limits imposed—and required—by situations controlled for study seem, in this instance, to run the gauntlet of peculiarity in a way which PCT methods may help to avoid.

In some respects, this area attracts even more readily than others this charge of artificiality. To some extent this problem is generally derivable from the fact that one is dealing with an individual's personal assessments of other individuals, and thus one enters the realms where social phenomena extend and become more distinguishable from other processes; for social perception is characteristically different from perception of other phenomena at some levels. For example, while it makes poor sense to talk of persons having two contemporaneous theories about the properties of inanimate objects, it is completely sensible to suggest that one can simultaneously hold two views of an action by another person and may wait to see which of the two views is ultimately the more useful (e.g. one may initially be unsure whether some new acquaintance is an 'ignorant idiot' or merely someone who is 'very shy and unable to communicate his thoughts adequately to strangers'). Equally, there are qualitative differences between the situation where one observes two examples of 'chair' and is able to say of a third item that it is a chair; and the situation where one observes two examples of 'generosity' and goes on to infer that 'This is a generous man'. The difference lies at the level of surety which can be attached to the induction, since the latter inference is no safe predictor of the person's behaviour on subsequent occasions. One may have been treated to two uncharacteristic displays of behaviour; he may be a deceiver; he may be a politician or an ingratiator. The flavour of Chapter 1 will no doubt return to the cognitive palate at this point, for it may be clear that the description of other persons involves entirely subjective issues, since objective measures of understanding another person can scarcely be provided. It cannot be claimed in objection that accurate prediction is a sufficient 'objective' measure, since individuals therein provide not only the prediction but also the criteria by which its fulfilment is to be ascertained (cf. Chapter 2, p. 25). Evidently, therefore, a social and intersubjective agreement is all that can be ultimately acceptable as a standard when it comes to the judgement of others. This kind of possibility must therefore be considered when attempting to avoid artificiality, and subjects' own descriptions assume an importance equalled only by the need to investigate similarities between them. Incidentally, some interesting questions can be extracted from implications of this discussion and will be dealt with later more fully. For it is a possibility that the ability to discriminate others and to evidence their predictions is held by individuals to differing extents. This raises questions about social skill, 'accurate' judges and the ability to perceive others, for the present theory is able to offer a particular kind of answer to the problem of what such phenomena are (see Chapter 12).

Indeed, in describing others, who have moods and emotions (which may perhaps be functionalized in PCT terms by reference to tides of selection of construct subsystems from within the whole), one will frequently be confronted with series of apparently inconsistent or strange behaviour patterns. But one has always available as a means of rationalizing such behaviour a vast range of superordinate constructs which may serve to harmonize the apparent inconsistencies (thus can *voltes faces* be explained by 'ambitious', 'moody', 'genius', etc.). Such superordinate constructs may add dimensions to the perception of persons which are not usually available for other kinds of description. Clearly, therefore, the fund of superordinate or psychological constructs available to an individual will influence and determine the range of his competences in social description. Similarly, one's expectations in this context may influence one's range of description and may prejudice selection of particular descriptions. Rosenthal's (1963) suggestion that an experimenter may be influenced by his expectancies has sure parallels in other social contexts. This may be true not only at such specific levels as that where A expects B to act like a 'fool' (and thus to fall into subsystem X of his construct system) and finds that he does. It also applies to the level of metatheory and to A's general views on how life may be ordered—whether he believes, for example that 'Opposites attract' or 'Birds of a feather flock together'. Such general outlooks may influence a person's perception of another by restricting the cues to which he attends.

It is thus apparent that this state of affairs creates two simultaneous general problems for the investigating psychologist. One of these is the recognition of the tenuous and socially based nature not only of individuals' descriptions of one another but also of psychologists' descriptions of individuals. This problem serves to establish once again the merit of studying individuals' *own* descriptions as the ultimate level where personality is relevant to the issues of interpersonal attraction. It thus requires that the psychologist's methodology be suitable to reflect such depth study. The second problem is to account for such possibilities at the theoretical level and to recognize the subtlety of the problems with which he is dealing, for they affect his notion of what is and what is not artificial in the laboratory study of social phenomena.

SOME METHODOLOGICAL ISSUES

Within the context of such general restrictions on the power of a theory to explain subtlety, there are specific points which can be made about the method adopted in these experiments. It is necessary to consider these before elaborating the theory further since they constitute the kinds of grounds on which even unelaborated theories may be criticized! It is therefore advisable to attempt a refutation of them as a preliminary to progress. For it is clear that this short series of experiments has been able only to confine itself to particular aspects of the theoretical structure. After the initial demonstration of the basic proposal that similarity of construct content was a differentiator of friendship from nominal pairs, the main purpose of the subsequent studies was to demonstrate the differences which occur in developing friendship and the stages which may be apparent. Under this limited head the empirical studies have demonstrated that such stages are discernible and that different kinds of friendship and attraction may be identified at extremely subtle levels.

However, in doing this the present studies have investigated the characteristics of a noticeably homogeneous population and while it is of interest to know about such populations in depth, it is also of value to test the width. The signs (Duck, in preparation) are that these stages *and* the effects of similarity are both identifiable in populations of schoolchildren from a very different social background. The enthusiasm to generalize from population to population is frequently overwhelming at this point in a book, but this caution may serve to cast the author's remarks into a perspective.

Other issues specific to the mechanics of methodology have been referred for comment in this chapter. In Chapter 6 it was mentioned that there are certain theoretical issues associated with the assumption made here that constructs are reversible (i.e. that so far as the content approach is concerned, 'Good–Bad' is equivalent to 'Bad–Good'). Mair's (1967) work on this point has already been noted (Chapter 5, p. 56) as showing that some subjects applied the negative pole of a construct in a way which included some elements that had previously been excluded. However, when the content of a system is considered, the particular nuances of particular applications of a construct may be held in abeyance and will clearly be more relevant considerations in depth studies of one individual where his whole semantic space and its systematic relationships are studied. Thus, in a complete analysis, this objection would be relevant against a methodology which attempted latitudinal study of individuals' friendships. In this particular case here, the answer to the objection is the same as that given to a related issue. In Chapter 6 it was pointed out that the present method adopts a different operationalization of similarity from that taken in many other approaches to this area. One method is to compare scores on the dimensions of a test, with the smaller arithmetical difference implying greater similarity; but as was pointed out above, two people answering the same set of 10 questions could both score 5 by answering each question in an exactly contrary manner. The value of this kind of similarity measurement would therefore seem to be limited and it makes more sense to tot up the similar answers to specific questions. But in adopting this kind of method as applied to dimensional personality tests or attitude scales one is depriving subjects of the personal elements which characterize PCT methods. In view of the outlook adopted previously, the attentive will find no inconsistency in the preference for PCT methods, which in this instance seem to offer improved access to the subjects' relevant processes. However, this advantage is the one which raises the problem noted earlier. Should one measure similarity of constructs, simply; or should one measure similarity of constructs *plus* similarity of application? The difference is the difference between counting 'Good–Bad' and 'Bad–Good' as similar or counting them as different. For while the two are similar in that the same words are used, they are different in the sense that the 'positive' pole in one is the 'negative' pole in the other. It could be argued that someone who saw 'Bad' as the positive pole was not really similar to someone who saw 'Good' as the positive, even if they both use the same dimension. Which then should the PCT methods use as the measure of similarity: similarity of dimensions or of assessment, given similarity of dimensions? Must friends agree or is it enough that they understand one another? Clearly, complete agreement is not only not necessary but also not likely, for we have started from the premise that no two adults are exactly alike. The hypothesis has, until now, been no stronger than that content similarities between friendship pairs will be significantly higher than between nominal pairs and there seems to be no reason to assume evaluative identity. In practice, disagreement on the assessment of a particular shared dimension is likely to produce dissimilarities of implicative structure throughout the system and to this extent is likely to decrease the number of other similarities which will be observed. Thus the two measures of similarity must tend to amount to the same effective index of construct overlap and so the use of similar dimensions alone would seem to suffice for our purposes when similarity of content is studied. However, the point bears on the later discussion of construct hierarchies and will reappear.

These methodological issues contribute specifically to the general background of caveat which attends the elaboration and development of the theory. For the extension of the theory will take place initially from the springboard provided by the three basic assumptions which the theory embodies (stages in acquaintance; emphatic fluxes in attention to cues;

evaluation and interpretation by the individual). It may already be clear that these convenient headings may suggest too plainly the compartmentalizing tendency which has been continually depicted here in disparaging terms. However, the three assumptions, while upheld in turn, have all indicated ramification and have demanded elaboration. For it is clear that the convenient separation of them becomes less and less distinct, but more and more suggestive of the view that they reflect parts of an intertwined and complex process. This produces such overlap in their domains as to impede the intuitive separation of the clear effects of each one severally.

PERSONAL INTERPRETATION IN A HIERARCHY OF CONSTRUCT CLASSES

However, it is on the final of the three assumptions which the elaboration rests essentially and it is that which is clearly integral to the other two assumptions. Its fundamental basis was that reality cannot be perceived without construal (another necessary simplification of a complex problem covered more thoroughly in Chapter 2). An extension of this view is that perception of objects comes ontogenetically to involve an (unconscious) act of construing or categorizing; and the 'reality' of everyday language is perforce a *construal* of the objects of our perception. The point is reiterated in order to impress the implications which it carries in this context, for it suggests that each member of a friendship pair or group may not only have his own personal reasons for forming a relationship, but equally that in doing so he may perceive (and therefore structure) evidence uniquely with respect to that relationship. It may therefore be clear that the desired theoretical integration may be extended here. For such a view would not exclude the effects of, for example, attitude similarity, complementarity of some needs or all the other offered explanations. The view here is a molar rather than a molecular one and can subsume the effects of such 'factors' by the claim that they are parts of an ordered whole, in the same way as is construct similarity. This means that although general rules may be discernible at one level to describe the operation of acquaintance processes, the process may retain something of an individual flavour accessible only to particular methods of enquiry. Of course, this point also has further implications, for it also reflects on the method used to classify constructs in these experiments and it will be taken up later in more detail. However, it alerts one to the possibility that failure subsequently to develop the simple original categorization (which divided constructs into Psychological, Role Interaction or Other groups) may possibly eclipse a more useful sophistication which may provide material for a 'general law'.

There is a further implication here which points to the need for scientific care in dealing with subjective interpretation of 'reality', and once more emphasizes links between the 'scientist' and the 'human being', for it is also something which is highly relevant in everyday interactions. The implication is that individuals may structure their behaviour repertoire differently as a function of their perceptions of either 'the situation' or the people in it (notable 'conscious' examples of this are to be seen in interviews, and when approaching a prospective father-in-law). Individuals may be led by this structuring to present markedly different images of themselves from time to time, depending on whom they are with, and, of course, those people then present may interpret the actions differently on this basis, just as they may anyway, given their own latitudes of interpretation of 'objective' phenomena. So Tom and Dick may have different impressions of Harry because Tom likes his black hair and Dick does not; or because Harry always behaves in a friendly way when he is with Tom, but structures things differently when he is with Dick and behaves in a domineering fashion towards him. (This, of course is another reason why the question 'Who was the *real* Napoleon? What was he really like?' is naive.)

It is in this context that the work of Rosenthal (1963) can again be amalgamated with the present view in a somewhat different sense. This broadening perspective indicates that individuals are able to impose on a situation not only their own interpretations of events but also distortions of the evidence about them and even some 'demand characteristics' on those with whom they interact. This is a reformulation of a point made in Chapter 1 with reference to the work of DeCharms et al. (1965) and Farina et al. (1968), respectively, whose studies make the point on the effects of subjective structuring of 'objective' evidence. The inference follows that individuals' construing as pure categorizing is not the only process involved in social interaction and interpersonal attraction, but that some other process is parallel to it and contemporaneous with it. As indirect evidence on this point, one can look to the suggestion of Stotland, Zander and Natsoulas (1961), who showed that similarity between subjects was generalized by them from similarity between musical preferences to similarity of choice of nonsense syllables! Taken with the earlier evidence of Chapter 6 that the *perceiving* of similarity is an important component of its functional effectiveness, this points to the importance of the parallel processes of evaluating what is construed and the inferences from it.

Similar observations have been made before but this statement of the position is important not only for the significance of the differences in its phrasing but also since it is derivable from a set of premises from a new standpoint. Schrauger and Altrocchi (1964) put the similarities thus in a tangential context: 'While the process of forming an impression may be perceived as an immediate unitary phenomenon, this process can be usefully conceptualized as consisting of three phases: selecting cues, drawing inferences about personal characteristics from these cues, and translating one's impression into an overt verbal response' (p. 301). In view of the suggestions of the earlier experiments here, the significant omission from this contention is of the process of *evaluating* that which is perceived, which may be logically prior or parallel to the drawing of inferences. For clearly the evaluation of a cue implies the fitting of it to a context, which inevitably supplies natural inferences, which in turn inevitably assist the evaluation. Some inferences are integral parts of the evaluation process and derive from the context which is implied while others follow well after the evaluation has been made and as the information becomes more particular and individual, and the 'data' are put into a perspective with its own implications. In either case, the result of viewing inference and evaluation as contemporaneous processes is, in the present terms, that either the inferences drawn from the 'data' or the evaluation of them may change with the proposed changes in the focus of attention, which differentiate this theory from those which claim a consistent and single-minded strategy with a single focus throughout. But these changes and the evaluations themselves are dependent on the movements made by means of or within the inferential structure. In other words the individual's pre-existing inferential structure imposes limits on the kind of hypotheses which he can erect from early construal and may even define the extent to which understanding of the other person is possible. This view gives functional significance to Kelly's insistence (Kelly, 1969, 1970, passim) that Personality Theories (or other theories), especially applied here to an individual's constructional theories, must be fertile. In the present terms, a fertile system would facilitate descriptive inference and therefore the progression through the hypothesized stages of attention to cues. This has implications for further research based on the present rationale and will be discussed later.

The extension of this view provided by the present series of studies rests upon the recognition of the things which, in this light, can count as a cue for individuals. Evidence was presented in Chapters 6, 7 and 10 that similarity of constructs is found between friends, and that subjects perceive the similarity (Chapter 6) and this invites the inference that evaluation of construct systems for similarity is occurring. In terms of the filtering theory, it has been argued that evaluation of construct systems acts as the final filter in friendship formation. The shift away from a major concern with construal of another's behaviour (or interaction style) towards construal of his construct system marks an important change of emphasis and is also the stage where the greatest differences are possible between individuals; for evidence becomes less plain, and the use made of it becomes less restrained and more dependent on the system of the construer. For it is here that there is the greatest disagreement on what counts as an act of a particular type. Arguments on whether people are tall or short are inevitably less time-consuming than arguments on whether they are shy; which in turn are less time-consuming than arguments on whether they are ambitious. These examples represent progression in the present terms and at each step the 'evidence' becomes different and more open to personal and peculiar interpretation. It is thus possible for the subjective interpretation of 'events' at these late stages to be less restrained and more dependent on personal uses of language. It may then be all the more unusual (and, therefore, all the more significant) to find someone whose interpretations of this kind of event are substantially similar to one's own. Hence the value of similarity in psychological construing for the development of friendship. Not only are a system's peculiarities most likely to appear here, for the reasons above, but a construal of those of another person's peculiarities that are observable at this level is therefore essential for an individual seeking to test for construct similarity in his everyday dealings. However, the method of inference to another's psychological constructs is shaky perforce, if the sole basis is the evidence available early on, and the more evidence gathered the more safely can the inferences be grounded and corroborated. Given this situation, the best plan for the individual would seem to be to gather different kinds of information at different points in acquaintance and to use this to promote a tentative and careful graduation along a hierarchical system of constructs and inferences. Indeed, it appears from the evidence of Chapters 9 and 10 that this strategy is often realized.

Might suggestions on the conceptual differences in types of construct give us the basis for a theoretical analysis of a hierarchy of constructs? Might this proposal give us the means with which to revisit social relationships in the G.O.W.? It is possible to offer some tentative intuitions on the possible kinds of construct types which exist, and thereby to broaden the categorization system which has been adopted hitherto. By viewing these kinds as linked in a hierarchy (in a sense which implies progression upwards, rather than simple interconnection) one is encouraged to speculate (Chapter 12) on the way in which social relationships may be conceived.

Inevitably, the hierarchy to be proposed below will be seen to be an oversimplification which will clearly bear further study and elaboration. Given this proviso, the progression suggested by these studies appears to be on lines which reflect very closely the types of 'social reality' proposed in Chapter 1 (p. 10). These were seen as the basic elements of social relationships and depended to a large degree on conceptual distinctions between the kinds of evidence which satisfactorily supported them. In like manner, the proposed hierarchy of constructs reflects differences in the kinds of evidence which are adequate for each kind of construct and suggests both a 'basic' type (where doubt is preempted by reliance on general linguistic definition) and also a purely evaluative and less stable or robust type (where evidence is more shaky and embodies a grasp of psychological processes). Parallels may also appear between the progression in acquaintance and the progression in ontogeny.

Specifically, the most basic level of construing will simply reflect recognition that the object, person, cue, etc., is there to be described. This in itself presumes that the individual's construct system contains within its structure the ability to differentiate this object, person, cue, etc., from the rest of the world. Some persons may lack the apparatus to differentiate some kinds of cue, while others may not find it functionally valuable to do so. For example, a colourblind person may be unable to differentiate red and green; 'normal' people may be unable to impose certain possible and potentially useful categorizations on nature, as in the case of those without absolute pitch; Englishmen do not make distinctions about snow which are clearly apparent to Eskimos. Similarly, one may go on to argue that there may be those who are 'interactionally colourblind', as it were, and are not able to recognize certain cues in others' behaviour.

This level of construing is not entirely distinct from, nor entirely identical to, the level where differentiations are given linguistic labels which are widely held and seldom disagreed with. Not all construing is verbalized or verbalizable, but within the domain of verbalized constructs there will be those where agreement is high and those where it is not. In the former group will be those which denote physical characteristics—an early cue, in our terms, for acquaintance. This is not to deny that agreement on the cue's description will sometimes be less than total, but most often the arguments which occur will reflect disagreements about what is to be made of the cue—its implications (e.g. whether long hair implies laziness)—or else will be 'border disputes' (e.g. 'Is his hair light black or dark brown?'). At one level, such disputes may indicate cultural or subcultural biases, but the level of cultural-normative construing begins more clearly with the cues which derive from non-verbal communication and the rules about the *kind* of behaviour which may be expected. Here the interaction cues and their implications assume importance as the construer moves to a concern over interaction style (Chapter 8). In this instance, cultural prescriptions about how to behave may begin to mingle with personal predilections and, while this merger evolves, the other person may be simultaneously construed, categorized and evaluated both in terms of his standing *vis-à-vis* standards of 'acceptability' at large and in terms of his fulfilment of the construer's preferences. A further but more sophisticated concern over the *kind* of behaviour which is to be expected may be found to materialize in role construing. Essentially this relates to summaries of persons' behaviour on the basis of the general classes to which they are seen to belong. This kind of construing inevitably is a very broad class which spills over into and even subsumes some of the other classes. However, one is making predictions about the person from one's knowledge or beliefs about general characteristics and thus the constructs enshrine more specific implications and predictions than some of those previously discussed. The extent to which the person is seen to conform to the expectations associated with his perceived role may imply a very definite kind of expectancy about his psychological construing for example. The wide class of psychological constructs centres on some grasp of what the other is up to. Here it is clearest that a vast number of levels of construing becomes possible. This serves to emphasize the point that the general and essentially facile way in which the hierarchy has been proposed may obscure the variety which may be present under each class term. Role constructs and psychological constructs must embody many levels and kinds. Evidently the hierarchy needs to be examined and explored both empirically and theoretically.

However, it is clear from the experiments and the hypothesis which has come from them that the observed progression up the hierarchy (in whatever form it is conceptualized) during the construal of others involves the broad process of progression from viewing them in terms of 'stereotypes' to a greater individuation and differentiation of them. A first crude perception in terms of personal stereotypes is clearly the easiest and, in some sense, the best method for classifying new acquaintances. For at this point there is no evidence to indicate the other's individuality, nor the minute ways in which he differs from others who have attracted similar gross labels, such as are attributed early on (see Chapter 8). Even the assumption (reported to be frequently found, e.g. Bieri, 1955; Fancher, 1966) that newly met others are or will be found to be similar to oneself involves a form of stereotyping which makes inferences easier by importing the framework of a prearranged fabric. Each progression in the system narrows down and particularizes an aspect of the stereotype to variegate and individualize one's view of the other person. This, paradoxically, seems (from the evidence in Chapter 9 on the use made of simple information) to require more frequent use of superordinate constructs (which are themselves more *general* in the sense that they represent wider categories, are more implicative and are more combinatorial). The specificity and individuation are achieved by placing the individuals in N-dimensional space, with the dimensions provided by the totality of applied subordinate and superordinate constructs. Stereotypes may be suggested by earlier construing, but do not place 'accurately' in terms of dimensions which have the most useful and frequent meanings for the individual's system. The reason is that after early construing the relationship of the applications of implied and inferred construct labels cannot, at that stage, be adequately known. Later evidence presumably helps to make more particular coordination possible within a subject's construct system.

IMPLICATIONS OF THE FILTERING HYPOTHESIS

It would be less than the truth to assume that these proposed stages are clearly defined or in any way of a unitary character. It has been the most convenient formulation but the suggestion is not that there are any clear cut-off points, nor that one process only is occurring at any one 'stage', but phenomena can be usefully construed in such categories for the purpose of conceptualizing their nature. Nevertheless, whatever detailed classifications are imposed it is clear that while there are gross differences between first acquaintance and friendship, it is not adequate to view this as a complete picture. Clearly there are intermediate differences between the two extremes. The possible usefulness of a more complex conceptual structuring must be judged for itself.

One advantage of the filtering hypothesis of acquaintance appears to be that it simultaneously offers an immediate and active explanation of why friendships fail. There appears to have been virtually no work on why established friendships break down nor has there been explanation of why it is that not all acquaintances become friends, as a topic in its own right. Explanations have previously been concerned with those situations where attraction is reported and it is *im*plicit that the independent variable of study was not present in sufficient strength in those cases where attraction was not reported. Filtering theory assumes more active processes than this: filters do not lead to low levels of attraction by their (passive) absence but by their (active) presence; they 'cause' attraction to be at a low level, in the same way as it is 'caused' to be at a high level when it is recorded. This is one of the implications of the observation that all social situations are potential bases for friendship, unless some filter operates to discourage its realization (Chapter 3). The explanation offered by filter theory is thus that breakdown of the progression in acquaintance occurs by means of and during the same processes which build them up, and that the casualties of experience are due to failure to meet an evaluative filtering criterion. Thus, distance is an initial obstruction to acquaintance; but negative evaluation of interaction style, for example, (or the realization that cognitive similarity does not exist, or some other filters) may have the same effect at later stages.

Similarly and conversely, interaction forced by proximity may sustain the view that initial filtering was 'correct', or may present the opportunity for the discovery that previous filtering processes have unfortunately 'eliminated' an individual who would have passed through later filtering, if allowed to reach that stage (this is the 'He's not really such a bad chap, after all' experience). For the operation of processes of inference from early information introduces the probability of error; and a possible consequence of erroneous (and negative) inferences would be the exclusion of a potential friend, while subsequent denial of the force of a filter may reverse its effect. On a practical level, one is left wondering if the reported rapid turnover in teenage romances may be due in part to the newness of psychological construing (if Little, 1968, is right to argue for ontogenetic development of construing such that psychological constructs develop with adolescence). This may result in novelty and insecurity of the implicative structure of such superordinate constructs, which may lead to weaknesses in the system. 'Faulty' extrapolation and inference in such systems could be expected to be more frequent than in adult systems and may lead more frequently to expectations of cognitive similarity than are discovered to be justified. This possibility, however, could at most be only a part of the reasons for high turnover and instability in such relationships.

Such considerations pose the question of whether there is a point at which filtering ceases. The view taken here is that, like construing, it continues even after friendships have formed, but that their formation and stability is ultimately dependent on the discovery of similarity of construing. However, the level at which this similarity lies is not entirely clear. From the results of Experiment E it would appear that it is, at least in part, similarity of particular constructs which is of importance, but the difficulty is whether this particular similarity is part of a wider picture and therefore only a contributory component of attraction or is a sufficient 'cause' in itself. In effect it also reiterates the question of the *levels* of similarity which are important. The same question could be posed of studies on attitudes. Is attitude-similarity claimed to be of importance because particular attitudes are consensually validated or because similarity of particular attitudes implies the possibility of an overall similarity of outlook? For workers on attitude-similarity to concede the latter possibility would be to concede the primary importance of attitudes. Yet the approach adopted here endorses the view that particular similarities are important because of the implications which they have for the similarity of the overall system. Yet this is not sufficiently precise and is perhaps too simple a view. A more specific claim would be that the similarity implied by similarity of particular constructs is a similarity of inferential techniques within an overall similarity of elements. However, even this is not enough, for the early arguments (and evidence to support them) all point to the probability that, while similarity of this sort is important, some account must be taken both of evaluations of other aspects of another person and of the relative weights given to them. It is not implicit in the acceptance of another for a friend that one will evaluate positively all of his acts (or constructs), nor that all will be similar. It is here that individual structuring of the relative importance of elements of another person will present the greatest latitude. Tesser (1971) has shown that both the evaluative and structural components of attitudes have implications for attraction and this may point to the further fertility of PCT which provides two parallel lines of approach. The structural line was earlier abandoned (Chapters 5 and 6) in favour of the content approach, since it was inadequate on its own because its methods tended to relegate content of meaning to the status of an epiphenomenon. Nevertheless, a fruitful line of enquiry may devolve on an amalgamation of these two methods, either in conjunction with or independently of further work on content alone. The further usefulness of PCT is thus open to empirical test, but the results presented here have offered a possible means of uniting different spheres of social psychology into an overall personality theory and thus offer a link between major theoretical and experimental areas.

12

Social Relationships Revisited

One of Kelly's claims was that the usefulness of a construct system is limited by its permeability (i.e. its ease of subsuming new phenomena and restructuring itself) and this can be seen to apply both at the personal level of construct systems and equally at the higher level of any theoretical construct system. The fertility of the present system can thus be seen to be limited as a function of its flexibility; the facility with which it encourages reconsideration of established phenomena; and the functionalization of its approach, in the relationships of the outside world. These three aspects of a system's fertility will constitute the final parts of the case argued here and will be seen to bring us full circle.

The first of these aspects promotes reconciliation of the two divaricate methods of PCT enquiry; for the functionalization of the proposed hierarchy of constructs is a prerequisite for clarification of the types of process involved in the developmental stages of acquaintance and to effect this it may be necessary to return to study of the structure of construct systems. But while the content method (i.e. the concentration on the actual content of constructs) on its own is preferable to the structural method (i.e. analysis by statistical techniques of the underlying structure of construct systems) on its own in this context, more may result from their conjunction on this specific problem. This amalgamation may be especially desirable in that it may simultaneously enlighten the relation between evaluation and similarity mentioned earlier (Chapter 11, p. 138).

The question of evaluation is plainly related to that of how filters are 'overcome', for in some cases individuals may indeed come to recognize that inferences drawn from cues were erroneous. Individuals may reconstrue the other person in a way which may involve devaluing the status of previous filters (as argued earlier). The relative values of an individual's filters and the contribution which each makes to the ultimate state of attraction may finally be treated best at a level where an amalgam of the PCT methods would be most productive (i.e. where an individual's content and structure may be examined), but in the preliminary stage some general principles can be construed to be associated with the progressive development of an acquaintance with someone. It remains to be seen whether an acquaintance skill (which enables the skipping or surmounting of certain filters, or which generates the kind of inferences which invariably assist prediction and understanding) could be discovered or induced on lines parallel to those suggested by Argyle (1967, p. 85). Indeed, the investigation of individual differences in friendship formation within this framework offers great scope for further study. To be more specific: the refinement of the category system for constructs may tell us more of an individual's style; but given the present system, a prediction is clearly that those who construe predominantly at the psychological level would be able to filter more quickly since they would be able to test and substantiate or reject predictions more rapidly at earlier times in interactions by applying superordinate inferences to 'trivial' information. They may therefore have a more developed sense of the relevance of minutiae to psychological construing. Such individuals would clearly have more scope for developing 'social skill'. Hearns and Seeman (1971) have shown in another context, with a different theoretical background, that subjects with high personality integration (a functional definition of some characteristics of effectiveness in performance) perceived more relationship between themselves and others; used more affect terms; used more approach and sharing terms; reported more positive affect; and used more diversified affect and behaviour terms. In the language of the present outlook, this means that more 'effective' interactors were more cognitively complex and construed in terms here classified as 'psychological'. This finding can be related to Bieri's (1955) report that more cognitively complex individuals were better able to predict the behaviour of others. That is to say, those who were cognitively complex were more fertile in drawing inferences to future behaviour. Adams-Webber (1969) extended this by the finding that cognitively complex subjects were better able to predict the *constructs* of a discussion partner. All of these findings are consistent with the view advanced here that greater 'psychological' construing is associated with greater inferential and social ability both at the stage of behaviour construal and when construal of constructs occurs. Clearly, then, there are differences in the abilities of individuals to grasp 'what the other person is up to'. This suggestion helps to clarify and operationalize Kelly's (1955) sociality corollary ('To the extent that one person construes the construction process of another, he may play a role in a social process involving the other person'). Kelly saw this corollary as having very far-reaching implications (Kelly, 1970), but it has been criticized for circularity on the grounds that construing another's construction processes is the definition of a role-based social process (Holland, 1970). However, it is extremely important to note here that the implications of the above arguments suggest that the corollary gets its operational sense from the four opening words: 'To the extent that...'. Holland (1970) claims that these restrict our ability to offer an analysis of such relationships as dictatorial ruler and duped subject, but there is no reason to be so pessimistic or to imagine that both partners in a social interaction play roles at the same level. The corollary may be seen to claim that the ability of an individual to play a role in a social process with another is defined not by the fact that he communicates but by the *extent* of his grasp of what the other is up to and this may differ in the two parties to an encounter. Those who do not fully understand *why* others do what they do cannot play full roles in social processes with them (although they may, of course, *think* they do, or may interact unsatisfactorily and may play a role *at a different or inappropriate level*). This may depend initially on the person's understanding of social rules, norms, non-verbal cues, etc., insofar as these give a shorthand guide to the other person's construct processes. After that, it will be ignorance of these processes themselves which matters. 'He told me he was a confidence trickster and, like a fool, I believed him!' Clearly such a person could interact with the other person *at one level*, but having no very clear grasp of what was happening, would be very likely to end up buying an encyclopaedia.

One's view of what a social relationship *is* will be affected by this argument (if indeed social relationships *are*. It may be a mistake of the same kind as asking 'Who was the *real* Napoleon? What was he *really* like?'). It would seem to follow from this position that social relationships must be defined in terms of the individual's viewpoint, such that two interactors may interact with one another but can be seen as having social relationships with one another at different levels simultaneously as a function of their different understanding of one another, i.e. *to the extent that* their respective comprehensions of each other's construction processes are qualitatively different. Thus the dictatorial ruler grasps the duped subject's construction processes to an extent that is more complete than is the subject's grasp of the ruler's processes, and to that extent they play different roles in social processes involving one another—indeed, the social process itself is qualitatively different for each of them. Such a position has interesting implications for the analysis of the components of 'social skill' and for several other areas of psychology (for examples, leadership; the interrelationships of demographically different social classes; the failure of personal relationships in mental illness; etc.) and for the world outside the ivory laboratory (for examples, marriage guidance; industrial relations; etc.). These ramifications will be taken sequentially in an analysis of the implications which the position has for one's view of social relationships.

Within the area which has been chosen for study here there are several concepts which can be revised in the light of the above suggestions. These revisions will be based largely on the hypothesis of levels of interaction and thus serve to challenge Holland's (1970) view of the unpredictive nature of Kelly's sociality corollary. On the contrary, it will be argued that this corollary does embody the exciting possibilities which Kelly foresaw and thus enables a somewhat different view of several phenomena which concern social relationships. But some of these views will depend on a ramification of the original 'holist' position.

Certainly, one can uphold the holist cause more justifiably by adopting the view that cues are evaluated. This renders possible a resolution of complementarity-similarity disputes mentioned earlier and promotes the integration of various different methods of studying the many facets of interpersonal attraction. However, the holist outlook also provides the means for an easy discussion of the relationship between this and other 'areas' and the ways in which each bears upon the other. For just as the linguistic aspect of social relationships may help our understanding of attraction, so too may the social aspect of language aid our comprehension of semantics. It is clear that the present approach has a concern over the meanings which individuals employ and a particular interest in the shared meanings which facilitate all levels of social encounter. Its links with semantics and linguistics are therefore not entirely tenuous. As such, the present view has links with Bernstein's (1958) views on class differences in language use and the view may therefore embody a relevance in industrial disputes (see below). This relevance largely centres around the kinds of similarity which may be discerned between systems. However, the view on the importance of evaluation has implicitly disturbed the simple suggestion of a 'similarity hypothesis'. For it is clearly possible to see this notion as far more diversified than is suggested by superficial perusal. Original ramification of the idea by the exploration of the obvious question: 'similarity of what?' seems at least to transmute into the question: 'similarity of what, when, for whom, to what end...?' The most valuable part of this question would seem to lie in the tail, since it is clear that the discovery of some form of similarity in association with high attraction levels may not offer a sufficiently complete picture The present outlook moves towards the view that some degree of psychological construing must be an inevitable component of social relationships, since it amounts to an idea of what the other person is up to. The inability ever to construe psychologically would inexorably disturb social relationships, even given an impressive background of similarity of other factors. Such an outlook is relevant to a view of mental illness (see below). Furthermore, since it has been argued that *extensive* psychological construing comes into existence only relatively late in development (not much before mid-adolescence, Little, 1968)*, this analysis predicts that friendship in pre-adolescent children will be of a functionally distinct sort from that encountered in adults. One may still retain the notion of filters to explain it, but one would require to stop short of similarity of psychological construing in one's explanation of what friendship means to a child. In terms of the present argument, one's view of the level of relationship which children may attain† would also be a matter for exploration (cf. La Gaipa and Bigelow, 1972).

These latter views emphasize the dynamic fluxes which characterize friendship and friendship formation, since new skills or new information or new cues are constantly presenting themselves to the interactors involved. Part of such processes may be the normative influences of developing friendship and stabilizing a relationship; for just as each interactor imports his physique to each interaction, and his interaction style to every meeting and his constructs to all relationships, so too are the preferences which are embodied in those constructs presented to the other interactor not only for cognitive analysis but also for reaction or absorption. The analysis of another's system need not stop short of the incorporation of some of the other's views into one's own system, nor need it exclude agreements on a compromise or a common course. Perhaps such possibilities as this are more readily available to the present approach than to some others.

Clearly that which is suggested above may require a recapitulation of the status and definition of consensual validation. While this notion has hitherto been a fundamental element of the basic position, it may be the case that (just as with the notion of a 'similarity hypothesis') the idea can felicitously be extended. In its original use here the idea of consensual validation contained an element of agreement about a particular evaluated item and this agreement constituted the available evidence for the validity of the evaluation. This idea may perhaps be too restricted. For some of the discussion in Chapter 11 raised the problem of whether similarity of fact or method was sought in constructs—i.e. whether agreement that Pole A

---

* At first sight this claim may seem a little surprising in view of the studies on moral development which suggest an awareness of 'motives' and 'intentions' as mediators of moral blame or innocence. However, further support for Little's work is to be found in Duck (in preparation) where schoolchildren of age 12 years used psychological constructs about 5 per cent of the time, and children of 14 years and $15\frac{1}{2}$ years had increased this percentage to around 25 per cent (still far short of the normal figures given on page 99 of this book). It would seem possible that an understanding of 'moral' problems is something more functional to developing children than is a more thorough understanding of psychological processes in other spheres. It is clearly an hypothesis supported by the work reported here that there are different *types* of psychological understanding. Moral understanding may be one of these types which develops first in the child as part of socialization, while other processes of psychological understanding may develop later as part of adolescence (i.e. becoming an adult rather than becoming a part of society).

† Conversely, it has been suggested that friendship processes may 'ossify' with ageing. (P. Kelvin, pers. comm.).

6—PR * *

('Happy') of a construct applied, or whether agreement that construct A–B ('Happy–Sad') was the correct dimension, however applied. The present case is a similar one. For one may require validation not only for specific views but also for one's overall method of arriving at and integrating them. Thus two individuals might validate each other's *meta*-constructs, without necessarily agreeing on how these meta-constructs should apply to actual construct subsystems. For example, two persons may be attracted because their thinking, their 'logic' or their method of arguing is similar. But they may actually differ on particular topics—they may *agree* to differ. Or one may apply his logic to one kind of phenomena (politics), and the other may apply it elsewhere (criminal problems). Similarly, the consensual validation position may be unduly restrictive in that it suggests a concern only over pre-existing cognitions. One of the benefits of a new relationship is the hope it proffers for the extension of one's experiences (both real and analytical) and it may be consensually validating to be presented with *new* information which does not conflict with pre-existing beliefs. Indeed, new ways of looking at old facts could also be introduced in a consensually validating matter—not as validation for one's view of the facts, necessarily, but as validation for some higher-order constructs. This kind of process may be part of what is involved in the 'normative' aspect of friendship formation referred to earlier. Some individuals may seek in others a way of extending and elaborating their own systems or may be looking for new ways of construction and action which fit, none the less, with a similar outlook. The possibility of such overall strategies as legitimate targets for test by consensual validation may have been obscured so far, because this kind of level has not yet been extensively surveyed. The *content* of beliefs rather than higher level *structure* has been most often studied. But the overall structure of beliefs and personality may be one element of real life social relationships which has been missed in the reduction of phenomena by studying the component, smaller units (see Chapter 3). It is a version of 'the wood and the trees' problem.

A further strategy (which is clearly in need of consideration in subsequent studies in this area) suggests the value of reflecting closely on the kind of social relationship which exists between the sexes. The findings reported passim here on the differences and similarities between strategies of friendship formation in the two sexes would suggest the folly of too firm a belief that relationships from the female's aspect are always at the same level as those from the aspect of the male participant. (It is clear that one is talking about *level* of relationship in a sense which has been extracted in the previous discussion.) One is familiar, of course, with the belief that women possess 'female intuition', and it may be possible to operationalize this suggestion in a close examination of the levels at which relationships may be conducted. This kind of development of interest would perforce accompany any investigation of the hierarchy of constructs considered earlier.

The identification of levels of relationship may mark a parallel to the 'stages' of acquaintance discussed earlier. These may prove to be crude and rather gross pointers to a fine grading of levels of relationship which may occur once the level of construct similarity has been realized. The results of Chapter 7 begin to suggest the feasibility of this remark, and the sex-difference findings offer some support. The importance of testing this suggestion need hardly be emphasized since it is at once relevant to the fields of Marriage Guidance and to one's concept of some factors in mental illness. Insofar as the strategies of marital partners and the possible levels of interaction must limit the extent of their compatibility, it will be important for counsellors to identify such differences with a view to their reconciliation (in two referents of 'their'!). Similarly, those mental disturbances which are related to the failure of personal relationships may be more readily treated in the knowledge of the gaps in the patient's social abilities. This kind of suggestion invites reconsideration of the ways in which mental illness may be related to the inability to establish or maintain adequate social relationships. If one is justified in the assumption that psychological construing is necessary for the generation and continuation of personal relationships, then this should be where mental illness might sometimes be founded. Insofar as differences in social skill have been postulated above, then one may suppose that these differences would be clearly marked between those with personal difficulties and those of a normal frame of mind. In short, one would suppose that those who experienced difficulties with personal relationships may be found to have less adequate banks or types of psychological constructs. This inadequacy may be reflected not only in terms of numbers but also in terms of peculiarity: for a prediction of the previous discussion would be not only that such patients would have available fewer psychological constructs but also that such psychological constructs as they did possess would be markedly more unusual (in terms of type or flexibility in use) than their role, interaction or other constructs, in comparison to those derived from a 'normal' population. In support of this claim one can point to the work of McPherson (1972) and McPherson, Buckley and Draffan (1971) who have shown the deficiencies of psychological construing which characterize some forms of schizophrenia. Such peculiarities might restrict the range of levels at which the patients could conduct social intercourse. This view extends the argument (Argyle, 1967) that mental illness may be generated by an inability to operate with basic 'rules' about non-verbal interaction. Clearly, disturbances would be equally likely to occur in cases where individuals were unable to grasp the other 'rules' by which their fellows conducted their social relationships. For this inability would lead not only to puzzlement on behalf of the patient but also perhaps to rejection or special treatment by other individuals. Such a possibility may have been a contributory element in Bannister's (1965) findings that thought-disordered schizophrenics had construing patterns which were 'loose' (i.e. did not differentiate substantially between elements in the world) and that this situation occurred as a result of the serial invalidation of predictions made about the world and, presumably, the people in it.

The inability to grasp another's construction processes is clearly an accessory factor in disputes of many kinds, and may be relevant in industry. While this claim is hardly new, the present discussion does offer a perspective upon it which suggests a level of enquiry based upon the examination of characteristic modes of contruing. Class differences in construing have already been shown empirically with PCT methods (Warren, 1966) and this finding can be taken with present work to suggest that class relationships may be affected by such differences. The investigation of this claim involves two facets: first, the possibility that social relationships within classes are characteristically different from one another (for example, they may depend on different levels of construing); and second, that relationships between the classes are rendered difficult by construct differences. This latter suggestion has considerable relevance to the sphere of industrial relations and may point to one possible source of difficulty in communications in industry. Clearly, it also has close affinities with the suggestions of Bernstein (1958), but offers a different conceptual framework within which to operationalize such suggestions. These claims would require a considerable amount of empirical enquiry to substantiate their basis, but the study of interpersonal relations in this context has a secondary benefit, too. Clearly, if the basis of compatibility depends on similarity of construct processes, then the job of the personnel manager in selecting among applicants for work teams would be facilitated by the extent to which he had absorbed the tenets of Kelly's theory of Personal Constructs.

The prediction of ultimately satisfactory pairings on the basis of early evidence is, of course, a major functional aim of much research in this area. By aspiring to the ability to predict and to warn, psychologists have hoped to help individuals to avoid the extreme unpleasantness of unsatisfactory relationships, and thus to contribute in a very real way to the solution of problems encountered in everyday life. It can now be claimed that this hope is not entirely the dream of the mad scientist. The present studies and their theoretical developments have shown both that the fulfilment of this intention still lies some way in the future and, simultaneously, that it is a realistic aim to hold in view. The ability to predict must follow from a clearer understanding of the exact nature of the stages through which friendship develops, but demonstration that these stages exist is in itself a large step forward. Nor is this a mere theoretical issue which concerns only the laboratory academic, for friendship and personal relationships concern all of us throughout our lives. However, it is here that the psychologist's claim to help others meet its acid test. It is a claim which must be measured against the ultimate practical benefits which derive from the isolation of fundamental bases, mechanisms, stages and processes in the relationships which are the very fabric of existence.

EXAMPLES OF SOME CONSTRUCTS GENERATED IN THESE EXPERIMENTS, AND THE CLASSIFICATION TO WHICH THEY WERE ASSIGNED

Psychological constructs:

Very sociable	Shy
Ambitious	Not ambitious
Friendly, but not too much confidence	Too much confidence
Interesting, sensible and mature	Flamboyant, with childish outlook
Self-opinionated and moody	More consistent
Helpful and kindly nature	Selfish and bitchy
Interested in people	Interested in self

Role constructs:

Sing and play guitar	Can't do either
Teachers	Personnel manager
Religious people	No religious views
Male	Female
Family	Non-family
Went to same school	Went to different school
Same age	Different age

Interaction constructs:

Easy to talk to	More difficult to talk to
Good to talk to	Boring
Talkative	Quiet
Make presence felt but integrate well	Become an embarrassment
Warm	Aloof
Quick tempered	Patient
Didn't say much, but took general interest in discussion	Didn't appear interested

Other constructs:

Both stand a good chance	No chance at all
Know each other	Doesn't know either
Lusty	Looks impotent
Had a crush on them	Merely a father figure

Have taken part in show-jumping competitions	Just interested in horses
Will soon be in teaching profession	Bit of a dosser (intelligent mind)
Room-mates, young and in love	Can't imagine him in love

The inter-rater reliability coefficients for assigning constructs to categories are given in the text.

Appendix A

ROLE TITLES USED TO ELICIT ELEMENTS
(Experiments A, B, C, D, and F)

'Elements' are the objects, persons, etc., which are construed on the Reptest (see Chapter 2, p. 22). In order to assist subjects to find suitable elements for the tests which they completed in the above experiments, the following role titles were used:

(1) Father, (2) Mother, (3) Brother, (4) Sister, (5) Ex-flame, (6) Current flame, (7) Male friend, (8) Female friend, (9) Disliked male, (10) Disliked female, (11) Favourite teacher, (12) Self.

The elements used in positions 1, 5, 9, 12 were then repeated as the elements in the 13th, 14th, 15th and 16th positions. All role titles here therefore elicited personally well-known others as elements. Where no person fitted the role exactly (e.g. if the subject had no brother), then the instructions were that they should 'put the person who had most nearly performed that role' (see below).

(a) Role titles in Experiment E (first test):
(1) Father, (2) Mother, (3) Brother, (4) Sister, (5) Ex-flame, (6) Current flame, (7) Someone you would like to know better, (8) Someone you regard as successful, (9) Someone you think is a happy person, (10) Someone you worked or studied with at a particularly happy time of your life, (11) Someone you regard as a threat, (12) Someone you pity, (13) Someone you dislike, (14) Someone you regard as a capable person, (15) Someone you admire, (16) Yourself

(b) Role titles in Experiment E (second test)
On this occasion the first six role titles from the first test were used, and the last six were as follows:

(7) Self, (8) Someone you dislike, (9) Someone you admire, (10, 11, 12) Three personal friends.

STANDARD INSTRUCTIONS FOR THE ADMINISTRATION OF REPTESTS

When subjects had all been given a copy of the Reptest to be used they were instructed as follows:
'The test you have been given is known as the "Reptest" and it is a method

for discovering the ways in which people categorize others. You observe that it is split into different halves. On the left is a grid of columns and rows; while the right-hand side consists of a series of rows which correspond to those on the grid. At the top of each column is a space. These spaces are for you to write the names of the people you are to categorize. I will now read out a list of roles for people, and I want you to think of a person you know who fits into this role and to write his/her name (or initials) into the appropriate space at the top of one of the columns. If there is no-one who fits exactly (if you have no brother, say) then please put someone else who has most nearly performed that role for you. Also can you please use each name only once.' . . . (The list of role-titles, where appropriate, was then read out. The following instructions were not given until all subjects had completed their element lists satisfactorily.) . . . 'Those are the people that you will be considering during the test. Now what you have to do is this. You will see that in each of the horizontal rows on the left-hand side, three of the squares in the grid have circles contained in them. Thus, in Row One there are circles under numbers 4, 6 and 7. These circles indicate the persons whom you are to categorize in that row. In the next row the circles are in different places and you are therefore to categorize different people on that row, and so on.

This is how you do it. Find the three circles on the relevant row and look at the top of the columns where they occur in order to see who you are to categorize. Form a mental picture of the three people indicated and try to find a way in which two of them are similar and *at the same time* different from the third. For example, two may be short and one of them tall; two may be generous and one of them mean; or two may be Irish and one of them Scots; or two may smoke a pipe while the other is a non-smoker, and so on. There are lots of things you may think of and what I am interested in are the things *you* decide on.

When you have decided on your way of categorizing the three people, put the way in which the two are similar in the "Way Alike" column on the right-hand side of the grid; and then put the way in which the third is different in the "Way Different" column next to it.' . . . (The experimenter then gave a worked example) . . . 'When you have finished that row in this way, go on to the next row, and so on.

To summarize these instructions:' . . . (the summary was then read out and written up on to a blackboard) . . .

'(1) Find the circles on the relevant row;
(2) See who they refer to and form a mental picture;
(3) Find a way in which two are the same and *at the same time* different from the third;
(4) Way Alike column, Way Different column;
(5) Next row, back to step One.

Are there any questions?'

Questions were answered in accordance with the instructions and further worked examples were given if required, using the examples of constructs given above. Subjects were then allowed to carry on at their own speed.

Appendix B

SUMMARY OF THE STAGES OF ANALYSIS AND TREATMENT OF THE REPTESTS

(1) Preparation of individual Reptests (all experiments). This entailed the removal of all instances of constructs which exactly and literally repeated a construct on the same grid, so that only one example of each construct was allowed to stand (see Chapter 6, p. 61).

(2) Comparison of pairs of Reptests (all experiments except Experiment F and Experiment G, see Chapters 8 and 9).

(3) Similarity assessed according to one or two criteria:
    (a) Conceptual (see p. 61, Chapter 6);
    (b) Literal (see p. 79, Chapter 7).

(4) Similarities between all possible pairs of subjects recorded for all constructs: 'Similar' or 'Not similar'.

(5) Similarities with Friends and Nominal pairs recorded in matrices.

(6) Matrices of scores submitted to the various treatments required by the individual experiments (see text passim).

A fuller account of the method of analysis is given in Chapter 6, pp. 60–61.

References

Adams-Webber, J. (1969) 'Cognitive complexity and sociality', *Brit. J. Soc. Clin. Psychol.*, **8**, 211–216.

Adams-Webber, J. (1970 (a)). 'Actual structure and potential chaos: Relational aspects of progressive variations within a personal construct system' in Bannister, D. (Ed.), *Perspectives in Personal Construct Theory*. Academic Press, London.

Adams-Webber, J. (1970 (b)). 'An analysis of the discriminant validity of several Repgrid indices', *Brit. J. Psychol.*, **61**, 83–90.

Allen, V. L., and Levine, J. M. (1969) 'Consensus and conformity', *J. Exper. Soc. Psychol.*, **5**, 389–399.

Argyle, M. (1967). *The Psychology of Interpersonal Behaviour*. Penguin Books, Harmondsworth.

Argyle, M. (1970). *Social Interaction*. Methuen, London.

Argyle, M., and McHenry, R. (1971). 'Do spectacles really affect judgements of intelligence?', *Brit. J. Soc. Clin. Psychol.*, **10**, 27–29.

Arnoff, J., and Messé, L. A. (1971). 'Motivational determinants of small group structure', *J. Pers. Soc. Psychol.*, **17**, 319–324.

Aronson, E., and Linder, D. (1965). 'Gain and loss of esteem as determinants of interpersonal attractiveness', *J. Exper. Soc. Psychol.*, **1**, 156–171.

Asch, S. E. (1946). 'Forming impressions of personality', *J. Abn. Soc. Psychol.*, **41**, 258–290.

Bannister, D. (1960). 'Conceptual structure in thought-disordered schizophrenics', *J. Ment. Sci.*, **106**, 1230.

Bannister, D. (1962). 'Personal construct theory: A summary and experimental paradigm', *Acta Psychol.*, **20**, 104–120.

Bannister, D. (1963). 'The genesis of schizophrenic thought disorder: A serial invalidation hypothesis', *Brit. J. Psychiat.*, **109**, 680–686.

Bannister, D. (1965). The genesis of schizophrenic thought disorder: A re-test of the serial invalidation hypothesis', *Brit. J. Psychiat.*, **111**, 377.

Bannister, D. (1970). 'Science through the looking glass' in D. Bannister (Ed.), *Perspectives in Personal Construct Theory*. Academic Press, London.

Bannister, D., and Fransella, F. (1971). *Inquiring man: The theory of Personal Constructs*. Penguin, Harmondsworth.

Bannister, D., and Mair, J. M. M. (1968). *The Evaluation of Personal Constructs*. Academic Press, London.

Beier, E. G., Rossi, A. M., and Garfield, R. L. (1961). 'Similarity plus dissimilarity of personality: Basis for friendship?' *Psychol. Rep.*, **8**, 3–8.

Bernstein, B., 'Some sociological determinants of perception: An enquiry into subcultural differences', *Brit J. Sociol.* **9**, 159–174.

Berscheid, E., Dion, K., Walster, E. H., and Walster, G. M. (1971). 'Physical attractiveness and dating choice: A test of the matching hypothesis', *J. Exper. Soc. Psychol.*, **7**, 173–190.

Berscheid, E., and Walster, E. H. (1969). *Interpersonal attraction*. Addison-Wesley, Reading, Mass.

Bieri, J. (1953). 'Changes in interpersonal perceptions following social interaction', *J. Abn. Soc. Psychol.*, **48**, 61–66.

Bieri, J. (1955). 'Cognitive complexity-simplicity and predictive behaviour', *J. Abn. Soc.. Psychol.*, **51**, 263–268.

Bieri, J., Bradburn, W. M., and Galinsky, M. D. (1958). 'Sex differences in perceptual behaviour', *J. Personal.*, **26**, 1–12.

Black, M. (1972). *The Labyrinth of Language*. Penguin, Harmondsworth.

Bonarius, J. C. J. (1965). 'Research in the personal construct theory of George A. Kelly: Role construct repertory test and basic theory', in *Progress in Experimental Personality Research*, Vol. 2. B. Maher (Ed.), Academic Press, London and New York.

Briscoe, M. E., Woodyard, H. D., and Shaw, M. E. (1967). 'Personality impression change as a function of the favourableness of first impressions', *J. Personal.*, **35**, 343–357.

Broadbent, D. E. (1964). *Behaviour*. Methuen, London.

Broderick, C. B. (1956). 'Predicting friendship behaviour: A study of friendship selection and maintenance in a college population', unpub. Doc. Diss.: Cornell.

Brown, R. (1965). *Social Psychology*. Free Press, New York.

Burns, T. (1964). 'Non-verbal communication', *Discovery*, **25**, 30–37.

Byrne, D. (1961). 'Interpersonal attraction and attitude similarity', *J. Abn. Soc. Psychol.*, **62**, 713–715.

Byrne, D. (1969). 'Attitudes and attraction', in Berkowitz, L., (Ed.), *Advances in Experimental Social Psychology*, Vol. 4. Academic Press, London, pp. 36–90.

Byrne, D., Clore, G. L., Jr., and Worchel, P. (1966). 'Effects of economic similarity-dissimilarity on interpersonal attraction', *J. Pers. Soc. Psychol.*, **4**, 220–224.

Byrne, D., Ervin, C. R., and Lamberth, J. (1970). 'Continuity between the experimental study of attraction and real-life computer dating', *J. Pers. Soc. Psychol.*, **16**, 157–165.

Byrne, D., and Griffit, W. (1969). 'Similarity and awareness of similarity of personality as determinants of attraction', *J. Exper. Res. in Personal.*, **3**, 179–186.

Byrne, D., Griffit, W., and Stefaniak, D. (1967). 'Attraction and similarity of personality characteristics', *J. Pers. Soc. Psychol.*, **5**, 82–90.

Byrne, D., London, O., and Reeves, K. (1968). 'The effects of physical attractiveness, sex and attitude similarity on interpersonal attraction', *J. Personal.*, **36**, 259–271.

Byrne, D., and Nelson, J. (1965). 'Attraction as a linear function of proportion of positive reinforcements', *J. Pers. Soc. Psychol.*, **1**, 659–663.

Byrne, D., and Rhamey, R. (1965). 'Magnitude of positive and negative reinforcements as a determinant of attraction', *J. Pers. Soc. Psychol.*, **2**, 884–889.

Campbell, D. T. (1965). 'Ethnocentric and other altruistic motives', *Nebraska symposium on motivation*, D. Levine (Ed.) pp. 283–311. Univ. of Nebraska Press, Lincoln.

Canfield, F. E., and La Gaipa, J. J. (1970 (a)). 'Friendship expectations at different stages in the development of friendship', paper read to the meeting of the Southeastern Psych. Assn., Louisville, Kentucky.

Canfield, F. E., and La Gaipa, J. J. (1970 (b)). 'A multidimensional approach to friendship', paper read to the meeting of the Canadian Psych. Assn., Winnipeg, Manitoba.

Conan-Doyle, Sir A. (1966). *The Complete Sherlock Holmes Short Stories.* Murray, London.

Crandall, J. (1970). 'Predictive value and confirmability of traits as determinants of judged trait importance', *J. Personal.*, **38**, 77–90.

Curry, T. J., and Emerson, R. M. (1970). 'Balance theory: A theory of interpersonal attraction?', *Sociometry*, **33**, 216–238.

Darley, J. M., and Berscheid, E. (1967). 'Increased liking as a result of the anticipation of personal contact', *Hum. Relat.*, **20**, 29–39.

Davitz, J. R., (Ed.) (1964). *The Communication of Emotional Meaning.* McGraw-Hill, New York.

De Charms, R., Carpenter, V., and Kuperman, A. (1965). 'The "origin–pawn" variable in person perception', *Sociometry*, **28**, 241–258.

Delia, J. G., Gonyea, A. H., and Crocket, W. H. (1971). 'The effects of subject-generated and normative constructs upon the formation of impressions', *Brit. J. Soc. Clin. Psychol.* **10**, 301–305.

Dewey, J. (1938). *Logic: The Theory of Inquiry.* Holt, Rinehart and Winston, New York.

Duck, S. W. (1972 (a)). 'Friendship, similarity and the Reptest', *Psychol. Reports*, **31**, 231–234.

Duck, S. W. (1972 (b)). 'What should theories of friendship formation seek to explain?', unpub. manuscript: Univ. of Glasgow, Scotland.

Duck, S. W. (1973). 'Similarity and perceived similarity of personal constructs as influences on friendship choice', *Brit. J. Soc. Clin. Psychol.*, **12**, 1–6.

Duck, S. W. (in prep.). 'Personality similarity and friendship choices by adolescents'.

Duck, S. W., and Spencer, C. P. (1972). 'Personal constructs and friendship formation', *J. Pers. Soc. Psychol.*, **23**, 40–45.

Ehrlich, H. J., and Lipsey, C. (1969). 'Affective style as a variable in person perception', *J. Personal.*, **37**, 522–540.

Ellsworth, P. C., and Carlsmith, J. M. (1968). 'Effects of eye contact and verbal content on affective response to a dyadic interaction', *J. Pers. Soc. Psychol.*, **10**, 15–20.

Epting, F. R. (1972). 'The stability of cognitive complexity in construing social issues', *Brit. J. Soc. Clin. Psychol.*, **11**, 122–125.

Fancher, J. (1966). 'Explicit personality theories and accuracy in person perception', *J. Personal.*, **34**, 252–261.

Farina, A., Allen, J. G., and Saul, B. B. B. (1968). 'The role of the stigmatized person in affecting social relationships', *J. Personal.*, **36**, 169–182.

Festinger, L. (1950). 'Informal social communication', *Psychol. Review*, **57**, 271–282.

Festinger, L. (1954). A theory of social comparison processes', *Hum. Relat.*, **7**, 117–140.

Festinger, L., Schachter, S., and Back, K. (1950. *Social Pressures in Informal Groups: A Study of Human Factors in Housing.* Harper and Row, New York.

Flugel, J. C. (1950). *The Psychology of Clothes.* Hogarth Press: London.

Fransella, F. (1970). ' . . . And then there was one', in Bannister, D. (Ed.), *Perspectives in Personal Construct Theory.* Academic Press, London.

Freedman, L., Klevansky, S., and Ehrlich, P. R. (1971). 'The effect of crowding on human task performance', *J. Appl. Soc. Psychol.,* **1**, 7–25.

Gough, H. (1964). *Manual, California Psychological Inventory.* Consulting Psychologists Press: Palo Alto.

Gullahorn, J. T. (1952). 'Distance and friendship as factors in the gross interaction matrix', *Sociometry,* **15**, 123–134.

Hays, W. L. (1963). *Statistics for Psychologists.* Holt, Rinehart and Winston, New York.

Hearns, C. B., and Seeman, J. (1971). 'Personality integration and perception of interpersonal relationships', *J. Pers. Soc. Psychol.,* **18**, 138–143.

Heider, F. (1958). *The Psychology of Interpersonal Relations.* Wiley, New York.

Hoffman, L. R. (1958). 'Similarity of personality: A basis for interpersonal attraction?', *Sociometry,* **21**, 300–308.

Hoffman, L. R., and Maier, N. (1966). 'An experimental re-examination of the similarity-attraction hypothesis', *J. Pers. Soc. Psychol.,* **3**, 145–152.

Hogan, R., and Mankin, D. (1970). 'Determinants of interpersonal attraction: A clarification', *Psychol. Reports.,* **26**, 235–238.

Holland, R. (1970). 'George Kelly: Constructive innocent and reluctant existentialist', in Bannister, D., (Ed.), *Perspectives in Personal Construct Theory.* Academic Press, London.

Homans, G. C. (1950). *The Human Group.* Harcourt, Brace and World, New York.

Izard, C. E. (1960 (a)). 'Personality similarity and friendship', *J. Abn. Soc. Psychol.,* **61**, 47–51.

Izard, C. E. (1960 (b)). 'Personality similarity, positive affect and interpersonal attraction', *J. Abn. Soc. Psychol.,* **61**, 484–485.

Izard, C. E. (1963). 'Personality similarity and friendship: A follow-up study', *J. Abn. Soc. Psychol.,* **66**, 598–600.

Jacobs, L., Berscheid, E., and Walster, E. H. (1971). 'Self-esteem and attraction', *J. Pers. Soc. Psychol.,* **17**, 84–91.

Jellison, J. M., and Zeisset, P. T. (1969). 'Attraction as a function of the commonality and desirability of a trait shared with another', *J. Pers. Soc. Psychol.,* **11**, 115–120.

Jones, E. E., and Schrauger, S. (1970). 'Reputation and self-evaluation as determinants of attractiveness', *Sociometry,* **33**, 276–286.

Jones, E. E., Stires, L. K., Shaver, K. G., and Harris, V. A. (1968). 'Evaluation of an ingratiator by target persons and bystanders', *J. Personal.,* **36**, 349–385.

Kelly, G. A. (1955). *The Psychology of Personal Constructs.* Norton, New York.

Kelly, G. A. (1958). 'Man's construction of his alternatives', in Linzdey, G., (Ed.), *The Assessment of Human Motives.* Rinehart, New York.

Kelly, G. A. (1962). 'Europe's matrix of decision', in Jones, M.R., (Ed.), *The Nebraska Symposium on Motivation.* University of Nebraska Press, Lincoln.

Kelly, G. A. (1969). *Clinical Psychology and Personality: The Selected Papers of George Kelly.* B. Maher (Ed.), Wiley, New York.

Kelly, G. A. (1970). 'Behaviour is an experiment', in Bannister, D., (Ed.), *Perspectives in Personal Construct Theory*. Academic Press, London.

Kelvin, R. P. (1970). *The Bases of Social Behaviour*. Holt, Rinehart and Winston, London.

Kiesler, S. (1966). 'The effect of perceived role-requirements on reactions to favor doing', *J. Exper. Soc. Psychol.*, **2**, 198–210.

Koenig, F. (1971). 'Positive affective stimulus value and accuracy of role perception', *Brit. J. Soc. Clin. Psychol.*, **10**, 385–386.

Kogan, N., and Wallach, A. M. (1964). *Risk-taking: A Study in Cognition and Personality*. Holt, Rinehart and Winston, New York.

Kramer, E. (1963). 'Judgements of personal characteristics and emotions from non-verbal properties of speech', *Psychol. Bull.*, **60**, 408–420.

La Gaipa, J. J., and Bigelow, B. J. (1972). 'The development of childhood friendship expectations', paper to the Canadian Psychol. Assoc. Montreal, June, 1972.

Latané, B., and Darley, J. M. (1968). 'Group inhibition of bystander intervention in emergencies', *J. Pers. Soc. Psychol.*, **10**, 215–221.

Lerner, M. J., Dillehay, R. C., and Sherer, W. C. (1967). 'Similarity and attraction in social contexts', *J. Pers. Soc. Psychol.*, **5**, 481–486.

Levinger, G. (1964). 'Note on need complementarity in marriage', *Psychol. Bull.*, **61**, 153–157.

Lewin, K., Dembo, T., Festinger, L., and Sears, P. (1944). 'Level of aspiration', in J. McV. Hunt (Ed.), *Personality and the Behaviour Disorders*. Ronald Press, New York. Vol. 1, pp. 333–378.

Lindesmith, A. R., and Strauss, A. L. (1969). *Readings in Social Psychology*. Holt, Rinehart and Winston, New York.

Lischeron, J. A., and La Gaipa, J. J. (1970). 'Expectancy-confirmation and friendship', paper read at the meeting of the Canadian Psychol. Assoc., Winnipeg, Manitoba.

Little, B. R. (1968). 'Factors affecting the use of psychological vs. non-psychological constructs on the Reptest', *Bull. of Brit. Psychol. Soc.*, **21**, 34.

Little, B. R. (1969). 'Sex differences and comparability of three measures of cognitive complexity', *Psychol. Reports.*, **24**, 607–609.

Lott, A. J., and Lott, B. E. (1965). 'Group cohesiveness as interpersonal attraction: A review of relationships with antecedent and consequent variables', *Psychol. Bull.*, **64**, 259–309.

Macaulay, J. R., and Berkowitz, L., (Eds.) (1970). *Altruism and Helping Behaviour*. Academic Press, New York.

McKeachie, W. J. (1952). 'Lipstick as a determiner of first impressions of personality', *J. Soc. Psychol.*, **36**, 241–244.

McPherson, F. M. (1972). ' "Psychological" constructs and "psychological" symptoms in schizophrenia', *Brit. J. Psychiat.*, **120**, 197–198.

McPherson, F. M., Buckley, F., and Draffan, J. (1971). ' "Psychological" constructs, thought-process disorder and flattening of affect', *Brit. J. Soc. Clin. Psychol.*, **10**, 267–270.

Mair, J. M. M. (1967). 'Problems in Repertory grid measurement: (1) the use of bipolar constructs', *Brit. J. Psychol.*, **58**, 261–270.

Mair, J. M. M. (1970). 'Psychologists are human, too', in Bannister, D. (Ed.), *Perspectives in Personal Construct Theory*, Academic Press, London.

Mann, P. A. (1971) 'The effects of anxiety and defensive style on some aspects of friendship', *J. Pers, Soc. Psychol.*, **18**, 55–61.

Marlowe, D., and Gergen, K. J. (1970). 'Personality and social behaviour', in Gergen, K. J., and Marlowe, D. (Eds.), *Personality and Social Behaviour*. Addison-Wesley, Reading, Mass.

Maslow, A. H. (1953). 'Love in healthy people', in Montagu, A. (Ed.) *The Meaning of Love*. Julian Press, New York.

Mead, G. H. (1934). 'Mind, self and society', in *Mind, Self and Society*. Morris, C. (Ed.). University of Chicago Press, Chicago.

Mehrabian, A. (1971). *Silent Messages*. Wadsworth, Belmont, Calif.

Menges, R. J. (1969). 'Student–instructor cognitive compatibility in the large lecture class', *J. Personal.*, **37**, 444–459.

Miller, A. G. (1969). 'Amounts of information and stimulus valence as determinants of cognitive complexity', *J. Personal.*, **37**, 141–157.

Miller, A. G. (1970). 'The role of physical attractiveness in impression formation', *Psychonom. Sci.*, **19**, 241–243.

Miller, N., Campbell, D. T., Twedt, H., and O'Connell, E. J. (1966). 'Similarity, contrast and complementarity in friendship choice', *J. Pers. Soc. Psychol.*, **3**, 3–12.

Murstein, B. I. (1970). 'Stimulus-value-role: A theory of marital choice', *J. Marriage and the Family*, **32**, 465–481.

Murstein, B. I. (1972). 'Physical attractiveness and marital choice, *J. Pers. Soc. Psychol.*, **22**, 8–12.

Newcombe, T. M. (1961). *The Acquaintance Process*. Holt, Rinehart and Winston, New York.

Orne, M. T. (1962). 'On the social psychology of the psychological experiment: With particular reference to demand characteristics and their implications', *Amer. Psychologist*, **17**, 776–783.

Razran, G. (1950). 'Ethnic dislikes and stereotypes: A laboratory study', *J. Abn. Soc. Psychol.* **45**, 7–27.

Richardson, S. (1965). *Test booklet, Study of Values* (British edition) NFER Pub. Co.

Rommetveit, R. (1972) Paper to Social Psychology Section of British Psychological Society, Sussex, September, 1972.

Rosenberg, M. J. (1965). 'When dissonance fails: On eliminating evaluation apprehension from attitude measurement', *J. Pers. Soc. Psychol.*, **1**, 28–42.

Rosenthal, R. (1963). 'On the social psychology of the psychological experiment: The experimenter's hypothesis as an unintended determinant of experimental results', *Amer. Scientist*, **51**, 268–283.

Rosenthal, R., and Fode, K. L. (1963). 'The psychology of the scientist: Three experiments in experimenter bias', *Psychol. Reports*, **12**, 491–511.

Rosenthal, R., Friedman, N., and Kurland, D. (1966). 'Instruction-reading behaviour of the experimenter as an unintended determinant of experimental results', *J. Exper. Res. in Personal.*, **1**, 221–226.

Rosenthal, R., and Rosnow, R. L. (Eds.) (1969). *Artefacts in Behavioural Research*. Academic Press, New York.

Runkel, P. J. (1956). 'Cognitive similarity in facilitating communication', *Sociometry*, **19**, 178–191.

Rychlak, J. F. (1965). 'Similarity, compatibility or incompatibility of needs in interpersonal selection', *J. Pers. Soc. Psychol.*, **2**, 334–340.

Rychlak, J. F. (1970). 'The human person in modern psychological science', *Brit. J. Med. Psychol.*, **43**, 233–240.

Sartre, J-P. (1938). *La Nausee*. English translation by R. Baldick, Penguin, Harmondsworth, 1965.

Schachter, S. (1959). *The Psychology of Affiliation*. Stanford Univ. Press, Stanford, Calif.

Schrauger, S., and Altrocchi, J. (1964). 'The personality of the perceiver as a factor in person perception', *Psychol. Bull.*, **62**, 289–308.

Schultz, D. P. (1969). 'The human subject in psychological research', *Psychol. Bull.*, **72**, 214–228.

Secord, P. F., and Backman, C. W. (1964). *Social Psychology*. McGraw-Hill, New York.

Senn, D. J. (1971). 'Attraction as a function of similarity-dissimilarity in task-performance', *J. Pers. Soc. Psychol.*, **18**, 120–123.

Siegel, S. (1956). *Non-parametric Statistical Methods for the Behavioural Sciences*. McGraw-Hill, New York.

Slater, P. (1969). 'Theory and technique of the Repertory Grid', *Brit. J. Psychiat.* **115**, 1287–1296.

Stotland, E., Zander, A., and Natsoulas, T. (1961). 'Generalization of inter-personal similarity', *J. Abn. Soc. Psychol.*, **62**, 250–256.

Stroebe, W., Insko, C. A., Thompson, V. D., and Layton, B. D. (1971). 'The effects of physical attractiveness, attitude similarity and sex on various aspects of interpersonal attraction', *J. Pers. Soc. Psychol.*, **18**, 79–91.

Tesser, A. (1971). 'Evaluative and structural similarity of attitudes as deter-minants of interpersonal attraction', *J. Pers. Soc. Psychol.*, **18**, 92–96.

Tharp, R. G. (1963). 'Psychological patterning in marriage', *Psychol. Bull.*, **60**, 97–117.

Tharp, R. G. (1964). 'Reply to Levinger', *Psychol. Bull.*, **61**, 158–160.

Thibaut, J. W., and Kelley, H. H. (1959). *The Social Psychology of Groups*. Wiley, New York.

Thornton, G. R. (1944). 'The effect of wearing glasses upon judgements of personality traits of persons seen briefly', *J. Applied Psychol.*, **28**, 203–207.

Triandis, H. C. (1959). 'Cognitive complexity and interpersonal communication in industry', *J. Applied Psychol.*, **43**, 321–326.

Tripodi, T., and Bieri, J. (1963). 'Cognitive complexity as a function of own and provided constructs', *Psychol. Reports*, **13**, 26.

Tripodi, T., and Bieri, J. (1966). 'Cognitive complexity, perceived conflict and certainty', *J. Personal.*, **34**, 144–153.

Walster, E. H. (1965). 'The effect of self-esteem on romantic liking', *J. Exper. Soc. Psychol.*, **1**, 184–197.

Walster, E. H., Aronson, V., Abrahams, D., and Rottmann, L. (1966). 'Importance of physical attractiveness in dating behaviour', *J. Pers. Soc. Psychol.*, **5**, 508–516.

Walster, E. H., and Walster, G. M. (1963). 'Effects of expecting to be liked on choice of associates', *J. Abn. Soc. Psychol.*, **67**, 402–404.

Warr, P. B. (1965). 'Proximity as a determinant of positive and negative socio-metric choice', *Brit. J. Soc. Clin. Psychol.*, **4**, 104–109.

Warr, P. B., and Knapper, C. (1968). *The Perception of People and Events*. Wiley, London.

Warren, N. (1966). 'Social class and construct systems: An examination of the cognitive structure of two social class groups', *Brit. J. Soc. Clin. Psychol.*, **5**, 254–263.

Whorf, B. L. (1956). *Language, Thought and Reality: Selected Writings*. J. B. Carroll (Ed.), Technology Press of MIT: Cambridge, Mass.

Winch, R. F. (1958). *Mate Selection: A Study of Complementary Needs*. Harper and Row, New York.

Winslow, C. N. (1937). 'A study of the extent of agreement between friends' opinions and their ability to estimate the opinions of each other', *J. Soc. Psychol.*, **8**, 433–442.

Wright, P. H. (1965). 'Personality and interpersonal attraction: Basic assumptions', *J. Indiv. Psychol.*, **27**, 127–136.

Wright, P. H. (1968). 'Need similarity, need complementarity and the place of personality in interpersonal attraction', *J. Exper. Res. in Personal.*, **3**, 126–135.

Author Index

The index is classified by senior author. Junior authors appear only if they are also senior authors of other works quoted in the reference list and text.
References to the bibliography and reference section are shown in bold.

168

Subject Index